YELLOW FACTOR

HAPPINESS IN BUSINESS

NINE PATHS TO ACHIEVE BUSINESS GROWTH, PRODUCTIVITY, AND PROSPERITY BY CULTIVATING HAPPINESS

ROSARIA CIRILLO LOUWMAN
with STAN PHELPS

Published by *Wow Now Publishing*

Yellow Factor was earlier published under the title *Yellow Goldfish.*

Published by *9 INCH Marketing*

Editing by Lee Heinrich of Write Way Publishing.

Cover and layout by Rosaria Cirillo.

Illustrations: Flowers by Aafke Mertens (aafkemertens.com) and five senses by Kate Wilkinson (madebykate.com)

ISBN: 9789083082332

First Printing: December 2020 – Version 1.3 (Jan 2022)

Yellow Factor is available for bulk orders. For further details and special pricing, please email rosaria@wownow.eu

In memory of my father, Umberto Cirillo.

He taught me the love of learning and sharing knowledge,

the value of smiling, the importance of being grateful and having faith,

and he instilled in me the Don Bosco teaching that

sanctity is about being happy and doing good for everyone.

- Rosaria Cirillo Louwman

This book is dedicated to my father-in-law Fred Wills. He is a constant example of looking on the bright side of life and enjoying the moment.

- Stan Phelps

CONTENTS

ACKNOWLEDGMENTS

We'd like to thank everyone who inspired us, supported us, or provided feedback and examples during the making of both books, *Yellow Goldfish* and *Yellow Factor*:

Shawn Achor, Nailah Aljasmi, Gloria Belendez Ramirez, Tal Ben-Shahar, Jeanne Bliss, Chantel Botha, Elena Brambilla, Magali Branchu, Loretta G. Breuning, Juli Briskman, Brené Brown, Rien Brus, Saamdu Chetri, Azzurra Cifarelli, Daniele Conte, Cara Crisler, Giovanna D'Andreta, Alec Dalton, Gilles Domartini, Marjolein Droog, Matt Drucker, Heike Faber, Sole Fasolo, Mo Gawdat, Massimo Finelli, Pina Finelli, Annette Franz, Luis Gallardo, Michelle Gielan, Dan Gilbert, Sunny Grosso, Nathalie Hennequin, Lana Jelenjev, Alexander Kjerulf, Asha Lalai, Lord Richard Layard, Jennifer de Lange, Gail Logan, Conchita López Vega, Mathieu Louwman, Wout Louwman, Matthijs Lusse, Sonja Lyubomirsky, Chris Malone, Eduardo Masse, Oscar Mendez Rosa, Ellen Metaal, Manuela Morello, Yoram Mosenzon, Jennifer Moss, Jim Moss, Tommy Nordkvist, Susan Oudshoorn, Maria Pastore, Sudesh Pokhrel, Danny Peters, Jennifer Phelps, Tara Phillips, Giovanni Portaluri, Patrizia Premoli, Zipora Sarah Richman, Amber Rahim, Reineke Reitsma, Khedrup Rinpoche, Daniella Rubinovitz, Ricardo Saltz Gulko, Claudia Schalkx, Eleonora Spagnuolo, Bruce Temkin, Paul Terry, David Truog, Mary Tucker, Kathy van de Laar, Lex van Den Elsen, Marieke van der Laan, Sarah van der Wiel, Sigrid Van Duffel, Mischa van Gelderen, John Tukums, Ruut Veenhoven, Erik Vercouteren, Eva Visser Plaza, Theodora Voutsa, Rudi Wells, Mark Williamson, and Audrey Weinberg.

FOREWORD

BY JEANNE BLISS

When reflecting on the reason we are all in business in the first place – it is to improve lives.

We not only have an opportunity but, in my belief, a responsibility to leave people's lives in a better state than before we encountered them. As my Italian Grandma would say… "leave the room cleaner than when you entered it!"

Businesses that conduct themselves in a fashion congruent with the values of the people within them do so in a more joyous and prosperous way than most because their lens is so clear about how they will… and will not grow.

Leadership is about choosing. It's about enabling people to bring the best version of themselves to work. It's creating an environment where financial prosperity comes out of enabling people to thrive and deliver value. And it's about choosing to act and lead in a manner that creates a wellspring of energy and energized people.

In their book *Yellow Factor* (formerly *Yellow Goldfish*), Stan and Rosaria have provided building blocks to help us get to this elusive core that sets companies, and people, apart. And for me, this always comes down to leadership.

They prod us on to get our priorities straight—taking care of people first—and enabling the rest to follow. They focus on this as "happiness," which, for me, is the prosperity of the human spirit.

Too often, business actions that are not grounded in intent to drive toward happiness or life improvement can turn inward too quickly. But actions established with an acute awareness of their impact on lives become deliberate bearers of relief, grace, support, and in their grandest state…joy.

Yellow Factor is a hopeful book. We need it now. I applaud its writing and encourage you to find a quiet place to let its message wash over you. Then apply its lessons not only to your work but to every aspect of your life.

With kindness and respect,

Jeanne Bliss

Jeanne Bliss is a champion for human kindness in business, President of CustomerBliss, and Co-founder of the Customer Experience Professional's Association.

INTRODUCTION

BY STAN PHELPS

"[Gezellig] It stands for something or someone cozy, nice, homey, friendly, snuggly, fun, comfortable, or enjoyable... but no word can really sum it all up. It's a feeling rather than a word."

-- Shoshannah Hausmann, Founder of Awesome Amsterdam

I am indebted to the Netherlands for three particular reasons. It all dates back to August of 2000 when I relocated to the country from the U.S. for a new role with adidas International. I moved from New York City to Amsterdam to lead Global Sports Marketing for Tennis. After a month in temporary hotel accommodations, I settled in a ground floor canal apartment on the Herengracht near Dam Square. The next three years would change my life forever.

#1. A WORD WORTH TRAVELING TO HOLLAND TO GET...

The first reason I am indebted to the Netherlands is for a word. In my first few months of living in the city, I experienced the friendliness of the Dutch and their easygoing nature. The Dutch tend to be happy people. In fact, according to the latest Happiness Report,[1] the country is the sixth happiest country in the world out of 156. I thoroughly enjoyed hanging out with both expats and my new local friends. It wasn't long before I heard a strange word being frequently uttered by both groups. That word was "gezellig." The middle Dutch word is pronounced *keh-sell-ick* with an emphasis on the guttural Dutch "g"

1 www.worldhappiness.report/ed/2018/

in the first and third syllables. It's hard to define this widely used word as it has a variety of meanings. According to Wikipedia[2]:

> Gezelligheid is a Dutch word which, depending on the context, can be translated as conviviality, coziness, fun. It is often used to describe a social and relaxed situation. It can also indicate belonging, time spent with loved ones, catching up with an old friend, or just the general togetherness that gives people a warm feeling. A common trait to all descriptions of *gezelligheid* is a general and abstract sensation of individual well-being that one typically shares with others. All descriptions involve a positive atmosphere, *flow,* or vibe that colors the individual personal experience in a favorable way and, in one way or another, corresponds to social contexts.

Gezellig is the word that most aptly describes a *Yellow Goldfish. Yellow Goldfish* are the positive little things we do to create an experience. Experiences that generate happiness for employees, customers, and society. Small things that create a moment and a distinct feeling of connection.

#2. A CHANCE MEETING BELOW SEA LEVEL

The second reason I'm indebted to the Netherlands goes back to December 30, 2000, when I was on a redeye flight from New York City to Amsterdam. While I was waiting in the baggage claim at Schiphol Airport, I saw a striking brunette standing at the carousel. Beyond her good looks, I had a strange feeling I knew her from somewhere, but I couldn't come up with where. I mustered the courage to approach her at 7:30 a.m. Here's how it went:

---

2 www.en.wikipedia.org/wiki/Gezelligheid

ME: "Excuse me, [awkward pause] this is going to sound like the world's worst pick-up line, [gulp], but I think I know you from somewhere."

HER: She sized me up and then started shaking her head side to side.

ME: "Do you live here in Amsterdam?" I asked.

HER: "I'm visiting my cousins and grandparents."

ME: "Do you live in New York City?"

HER: "No."

ME: Grasping... "Portland, Oregon?"

HER: "Nope."

ME: [Exasperated] "Okay...where do you live?"

HER: "Connecticut."

ME: Light bulb moment, "Aha! Jennifer Wills…we went to high school together at St. Joe's in Trumbull! I'm Stan Phelps."

HER: [Blank stare]

In a small world moment, I met a high school classmate. Jennifer and I were in the same homeroom our senior year in high school. Far from love at first sight, it was just exciting to meet someone from my old hometown. I explained I was living in Amsterdam, and she said she traveled over once or twice a year to spend time with family. I gave her my business card and asked her to look me up next time she was in town so that we could grab a coffee.

Fourteen months would pass. In February 2012, I received an email. Jenn had just recently been promoted at Carters. In moving to her new office at the childrenswear company, she came across my card. "I'm coming over to Amsterdam in two weeks. Want to get coffee?" That simple email started a courtship that spanned dates in Amsterdam, Paris, New York, Prague, Cape Town, Seattle, Edinburgh, and

Portland. In the Fall of 2014, we were married. Two boys, Thomas and James, followed in the next three years. Life has never been the same again. All because of a chance encounter at Schiphol Airport, the only airport in the world that's below sea level.

#3. CIAO, ROSARIA!

The third reason I'm indebted to the Netherlands comes by way of Italy. In 2017, I was deep in research for *Pink Goldfish*. As I typically do, I reach out to my network, asking for examples. One of my customer experience connections in the Netherlands replied via LinkedIn:

> Hi Stan, I hope you are well! I would love to connect further... Since your email, I kept daydreaming about co-writing a Yellow Goldfish book with examples of how companies contribute to happiness! Looking forward to hearing from you and maybe connect in a zoom call. Smiling regards, Rosaria

I was intrigued. Happiness and contribution have been constant threads throughout the Goldfish Series. The original book, *Purple Goldfish*, focused exclusively on customers. It quickly became apparent to me that customers were only part of the equation. I learned that the companies who got "it" for the customers, put an even greater emphasis on their employees. In the words of Ted Coiné in the foreword of *Green Goldfish*, "You can't have happy enthused customers without happy engaged employees." *Red Goldfish* explored how being "for purpose" drives happiness and adds a sense of meaning for customers, employees, and society.

I immediately researched Rosaria and was impressed with her background. She is the co-founder of the CXPA in the Netherlands and was the second person to become credentialed as a Certified Customer Experience Professional (CCXP) in the country. She is one of only nine CCXP Authorized Resource and Training (ART) Providers worldwide to help others prepare for the CCXP exam.

In addition to previous stints at Forrester and Phillips, she now headed up her consultancy, Wow Now.[3] Also, we were both TEDx speakers. Eighteen months earlier, she had delivered a TEDx talk on happiness at Tor Vergata University[4] in Rome. The talk focused on the concept of *Happiness Driven Growth,* a revolutionary business model. Rosaria believes that we need to redefine happiness in a business context and that happiness can and should be driving business growth. Companies can design and deliver remarkable customer experiences that enrich lives and enable fulfilling interactions for both customers and employees. And when they do that, customers buy again and again, to FEEL happy over and over again. This dynamic is the case for a growth model driven by happiness. Instead of chasing increased loyalty and profit, companies should maximize overall happiness.

We decided to move forward with the book project in 2017 with the launch of the Yellow Goldfish Project, a crowdsourcing effort on List.ly.[5] Based on nearly 300 examples collected, we created a framework for happiness driven growth, which we shared with the world with the publication of *Yellow Goldfish* in 2018.

In 2020 Rosaria made some revisions and additions based on new learning, which are included in this version of *Yellow Goldfish,* renamed *Yellow Factor*. Here's a short overview of the book.

---

3 www.wownow.eu
4 www.youtube.com/watch?v=ppvA3124asw
5 www.list.ly/list/1nzZ-yellow-goldfish-project

Yellow Factor has four main sections:

Section I outlines the **Why**. It explores the history and science of happiness and the background on the metaphor of a Yellow Goldfish and the Sunflower.

Section II showcases the **What**. We'll uncover nine keys for H.A.P.P.I.N.E.S.S: **H**ealth, **A**utonomy, **P**urpose, **P**lay, **I**ntegrity, **N**ature, **E**mpathy, **S**implicity, and **S**mile.

Section III explains the **How**. Here we share the process behind creating your *Yellow Factor* for Happiness and Growth: **G**rounding, **R**eaching-up, **O**perationalizing, **W**owing, **T**aking Time, and **H**arvesting.

Section IV brings us home. The book finishes with five main takeaways and suggested readings.

Ready to jump in? We'll start with how happiness plays into the evolution of business. Let's go...

SECTION I

OVERVIEW (THE WHY)

CHAPTER 1

WHY HAPPINESS

"...the function of man is to live a certain kind of life, and this activity implies a rational principle, and the function of a good man is the good and noble performance of these, and if any action is well performed it is performed in accord with the appropriate excellence: if this is the case, then happiness turns out to be an activity of the soul in accordance with virtue."

- Aristotle (Nicomachean Ethics, 1098a13)

THE EVOLUTION OF BUSINESS

"Why are we here?" is perhaps the most critical question of all. It has been pondered since the earliest days of human existence. It is our search for meaning in this world. Each of us is challenged with answering this question. Mark Twain once said that the two most important days in our lives are the day we are born and the day we find out why.

Should the "why" question apply to business as well? Why are companies in business? What or who is the first priority? Where is the main focus? We believe there are five schools of thought or different management approaches that companies have adopted over the past few decades.

We'll call the first school of thought the 1.0 version.

BUSINESS 1.0 – SHAREHOLDER FIRST

"There is one and only one social responsibility of business, and that is to engage in activities designed to increase profits."

- Milton Friedman

The 1.0 version of business is a shareholder first mindset. The sole purpose of a company was to maximize profits. The late economist Milton Friedman became its foremost proponent. In his 1970 *New York Times* [6] article, he famously shared: "there is one and only one social responsibility of business – to use its resources and engage in activities designed to increase its profits so long as it stays within the rules of the game, which is to say, engages in open and free competition without deception or fraud."

6 www.colorado.edu/studentgroups/libertarians/issues/friedman-soc-resp-business.html

Profit was the coveted prize of business. Friedman excoriated leaders who sought anything beyond profits as "unwitting puppets of the intellectual forces that have been undermining the basis of a free society." Business leaders who pursued social interests were guilty of spending money that wasn't their own. Friedman branded them as "unelected government officials" who were illegally taxing employers and customers. The simple goal of the business was to provide a return to shareholders. Focusing on external social responsibilities or lofty ideals would distract the business from its sole purpose of maximizing profits.

Figure 1. Source: Stan Phelps & Rosaria Cirillo

Friedman believed that doing good was incompatible with doing well for your shareholders. Over the last two decades, this view has been changing. "There is an increasing awareness that the purpose of a company has to go beyond shareholder value, and that this is not something that will cost your business but something that will enhance your business," said Michael Beer, Cahners-Rabb Professor of Business Administration, Emeritus, at Harvard Business School.

The next evolution of business puts the focus squarely on customers first.

BUSINESS 2.0 - CUSTOMER FIRST

"Not so long ago companies assumed the purpose of a business is to make money. But that has proved as vacuous as saying the purpose of life is to eat... The purpose of a business is to create and keep a customer."

- Ted Levitt

The 2.0 version of business sees profit as a result, not the goal. Companies should be dedicated to the business of getting and keeping customers. This focus places importance on the overall customer experience and managing ongoing relationships. In the words of Walmart's founder, Sam Walton, "There is only one boss. The customer. And he can fire everybody in the company from the chairman on down, simply by spending his money somewhere else."

The late Ted Levitt believed that companies should stop defining themselves by what they produce. Instead, they should reorient themselves toward customer needs. In his best-known *Harvard Business Review*[7] article, "Marketing Myopia," Levitt made a case for companies focusing on customers. He used the railroad industry to illustrate the point:

> The railroads did not stop growing because the need for passenger and freight transportation declined. That grew. The railroads are in trouble today, not because that need

7 www.hbr.org/2004/07/marketing-myopia

> was filled by others (cars, trucks, airplanes, and even telephones) but because the need was not filled by the railroads themselves. They let others take customers away from them because they assumed themselves to be in the railroad business rather than in the transportation business. The reason they defined their industry incorrectly was that they were railroad-oriented instead of transportation-oriented; they were product-oriented instead of customer-oriented.

Want an example of a company that puts its customers first? Look no further than Amazon. It's the focus of their mission: "We seek to be Earth's most customer-centric company." Founder Jeff Bezos puts customers first and profit second. "We're not competitor obsessed, we're customer-obsessed. We start with the customer, and we work backward...We've had three big ideas at Amazon that we've stuck with for 18 years, and they're the reason we're successful: Put the customer first. Invent. And be patient." says Bezos.

This obsession with customers dates back to the earliest days of Amazon. There is always an empty chair in company meetings. The chair at the table represents the customer. The message is clear; the current customer is always top of mind and seen as the most important person in the room.

As early as 1954, Peter Drucker made a similar argument for a customer-first focus in his classic book, *Management,*[8] when he wrote, "There is only one valid definition of business purpose: to create a satisfied customer... It is the customer who determines what a business is. It is the customer alone whose willingness to pay for a good or a service converts economic resources into wealth, things

---

8 www.amazon.com/dp/B0017LGUPU/ref=dp-kindle-redirect?_encoding=UTF8&btkr=1

into goods... The customer is the foundation of a business and keeps it in existence."

He also said: "Profit for a company is like oxygen for a person. If you don't have enough of it, you are out of the game. But if you think your life is about breathing, you're really missing something."

The next version of business puts employees and culture at the forefront.

BUSINESS 3.0 - EMPLOYEE FIRST

"Employees First, Customers Second is a management approach. It is a philosophy, a set of ideas, a way of looking at strategy and competitive advantage."

– Vineet Nayar, Former CEO of HCL Technologies, author Employees First, Customers Second

The 3.0 version of business places employees first. It's rooted in understanding where value is created in an organization. It's built in the last two feet of a transaction, the space between the employee and the customer. Former HCL Technologies CEO Vineet Nayar[9] calls these 24 inches the "value zone." Nayar made employees the priority at HCL, putting employees first, customers second, management third, and shareholders last. He believed front line employees were the true custodians of the brand and drivers of customer loyalty. Nayar wanted to shift the focus from the "WHAT" of what HCL offered, to the "HOW" of delivering value.

A focus on employees first is based on the idea that culture trumps strategy in an organization. The experience of your employees becomes paramount as it dictates your overall culture. "I came to see

9 www.forbes.com/sites/stanphelps/2014/09/14/southwest-airlines-understands-the-heart-of-marketing-is-experience

in my time at IBM that 'culture' isn't just one aspect of the game—it is the game," says Lou Gerstner, former IBM CEO and author of *Who Says Elephants Can't Dance*.

In today's workplace, up to 70 percent of workers are either not engaged or are actively disengaged. To be successful, you need employees who are engaged to create a strong customer experience. According to Ted Coiné, author of *Five Star Customer Service* and the foreword for *Green Goldfish*, "You can't create happy, enthused customers without happy, engaged employees."

The next evolution of business places purpose as the critical first piece of the puzzle.

BUSINESS 4.0 - PURPOSE FIRST

"On the face of it, shareholder value is the dumbest idea in the world... Shareholder value is a result, not a strategy... Your main constituencies are your employees, your customers, and your products."

- Jack Welch, Former CEO of GE

The 4.0 version of business places purpose first. Companies that have a robust and defined purpose find that it drives employee engagement, connects with customers, and fuels the bottom line. According to Deloitte Global CEO Punit Renjen, "Exceptional firms have always been good at aligning their purpose with their execution, and as a result, have enjoyed category leadership in sales and profits." John Kotter and James Heskett demonstrated in their book *Corporate*

Culture & Performance[10] that purposeful, value-driven companies outperform their counterparts in stock price by a factor of 12.

Purpose relates to your "Why" as a business. To quote Simon Sinek, "People don't buy what you do or how you do it, they buy why you do it." It should permeate everything you do. "Every decision should be looked at in terms of purpose. Some decisions may be purpose neutral. But purpose is certainly not just a marketing issue or positioning of your brand image. Purpose should impact every aspect of the firm," says Raj Sisodia, author of *Conscious Capitalism* and FW Olin Distinguished Professor of Global Business at Babson College.

Embracing purpose can become a driver of employee engagement. Daniel Pink touched on the importance of purpose in his book *Drive*. Pink said three things motivate people: autonomy, mastery, and purpose. He believes that purpose is perhaps the greatest of the three, because a definite purpose allows you to overcome obstacles and persevere toward a goal.

10 www.amazon.com/dp/B0033C58EU

A NEW WAY FORWARD – 5.0 HAPPINESS FIRST

It seems to us like the old millennial debate about what is at the center of the solar system—the Sun or the Earth.

Enter Happiness.

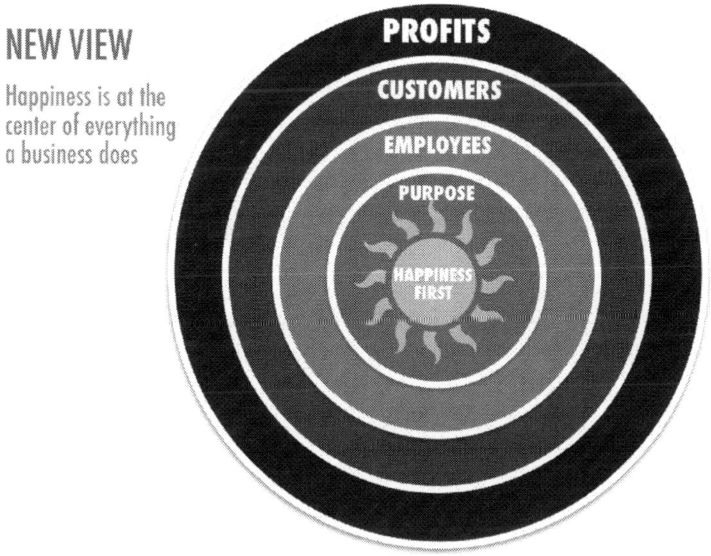

Figure 2. Source: Stan Phelps & Rosaria Cirillo

Happiness relates to our "Why" as human beings and to our shared goal as a living specie. About 2,500 years ago, Aristotle pointed out that if we apply "why" to any question, in the end, we find that everything we do has to do with wanting to be and feel happier. In Aristotle's words: "Happiness is something final and self-sufficient and is the end of action. Everything that we choose, we choose for the sake of something else—except happiness."

Happiness makes us thrive, fulfill our potential, achieve more, and live longer. Sonja Lyubomirsky, Laura King, and Ed Diener show us how happiness led to higher income, better performance, and better mental and physical health. In their breakthrough article "The

Benefits of Frequent Positive Affect: Does Happiness Lead to Success?*", they note: "Numerous studies show that happy individuals are successful across multiple life domains, including marriage, friendship, income, work performance, and health." The relationship between success and happiness is reciprocal; not only are we more successful, but our immune system is more robust.

Happiness is the ultimate WHY, the most sustainable competitive advantage, and the ultimate currency in the Purpose Economy. It offers a **competitive advantage** because we buy, work, and live to pursue and attain happiness; because we buy *more*, work *better and more effectively,* and live *longer and healthier* lives when we are happy. The search for happiness drives the choices we make due to the chemical wiring of the brain. Happiness is also the "**ultimate currency,"** as Tal Ben-Shahar calls it in *Happier*. He says, "Through evaluating how happy something makes us, we have a common currency that enables us to compare seemingly unrelated experiences."

We believe that we are at the beginning of a widespread realization that there is a version 5.0 of business which sees happiness at the center of what we do: happiness for the customers that we serve, happiness of the employees within the organization, and happiness at a societal level, happiness for the next generation. When happiness is at the center, and everything else rotates with purpose around it, profit, prosperity, and growth will follow as a result.

We'll look at both of these aspects in Chapter 2, but first let's look at the concept of happiness.

BRIEF HISTORY of HAPPINESS

The source of the word *happiness* is the Icelandic word *happ*, which means "luck" or "chance," and, interestingly, is the same source for *haphazard* and *happenstance.*[11]

If we look at the word happiness in other languages, we find a striking fact. In every Indo-European language, without exception, going back to ancient Greek, the word for happiness is associated with the word for *luck*. As examples, the Old French *heur*, root of *bonheur*, good fortune or happiness, just means luck or chance. German gives us the word *Gluck*, Dutch *Geluk,* which, to this day, means both happiness and luck.

What does this linguistic pattern suggest? For a good many ancient peoples—and for many others long after that—happiness was not something humankind could control. It was in the hands of the gods, dictated by Fate or Fortune, controlled by the stars, not something that humans could count upon or make for itself. Happiness, literally, was what happened to humans, and that was ultimately out of their hands. That thinking began to change with philosophers in ancient Athens who started to think that humans did have some control over their fate and their happiness.

Socrates, Plato, and Aristotle argued that happiness was up to people themselves. While they searched for happiness in different philosophical ways, they agreed happiness was worthy of seeking and within the human realm to find. Like Socrates and Plato, we believe that each individual is responsible for his/her happiness. Like Aristotle, we also believe that the world—including the business world—we live, exchange goods, and operate in can have a massive impact on our happiness and that organizations have the ability (dare we say responsibility?) to contribute to our happiness.

---

11 *Happier*, Tal Ben-Shahar

If we fast forward to the last century, we see that in 1943, Abraham Maslow developed the hierarchy of needs and coined the term "Positive Psychology." In the late 1980s, Mihaly Czikszentmihalyi launched "The Science of Happiness," the scientific study of "what makes happy people happy," pioneering the "experience sampling method" to discover what he called the "psychology of optimal experience" and specifically, the experience of Flow.[12] In 1998, Dr. Martin Seligman pioneered Positive Psychology at the University of Pennsylvania. In 2006, Tal Ben-Shahar's Harvard PosPsych 1504 course broke university attendance records, and in 2018, he launched The Happiness Studies Academy online as the first truly interdisciplinary course about happiness. The Academy now has participants from all over the world. The insights revealed by the modern "Science of Happiness" have remarkable similarities to the ideas of ancient thinkers such as Confucius, Buddha, Socrates, and Aristotle.

Since 2012, governmental actions embracing happiness are growing: the UN defined March 20 as International Day of Happiness; the Sustainable Development Solutions Network (SDSN) published the First World Happiness Report[13] (including a chapter dedicated to "Happiness at Work" since the 7th edition in 2017); governments have been adopted or are adopting various Happiness indexes and measures (like Bhutan's GNH – Gross National Happiness), and countries have named Ministers of Happiness; in 2018, the UK named a Minister of Loneliness (maybe some positive thinking and wording could have been considered here!).

Overall, we observe that Happiness research, discussions, and multiple movements have accelerated exponentially in the past ten years across universities, institutions, and governments around the world. And we see that the most innovative and forward-looking

12 www.pursuit-of-happiness.org/science-of-happiness/

13 In 2018 at its 8th edition available on www.worldhappiness.report/ed/2018/

companies have already adopted Business 5.0, pursuing what we call "Happiness Driven Growth."

WHY HAPPINESS DRIVEN GROWTH

Rosaria grew up in Caserta, close to Naples, surrounded by people who thought that life was about working hard, about sacrifice. They accepted the limited quality of life their city offered, the slow and malfunctioning public administration, and they didn't capitalize on the fantastic natural landscape or the local heritage, like the Royal Palace,[14] that surrounded them.

Everyone complained but accepted what Rosaria would call "mediocre experiences." It seemed that they had put a limit on their possible happiness. She didn't get it.

Wasn't the purpose of life to pursue happiness, as Aristotle had already concluded 2,500 years before?

"Why were we *(well, I did rebel!)* accepting mediocre services, and why weren't we using the treasures we had to maximize our happiness?"

To get answers to these questions, Rosaria left Caserta to study in Rome and embarked on a journey to understand Happiness through Economics—in the hope that there she could not only find the answers to her questions but also learn everything needed to drive a change.

In her final university year, Rosaria went to Amsterdam for an internship at Forrester Research while working on her thesis. It was then that she was captured by the "*gezellig*" way of living and working in the Netherlands. As Stan also experienced and explained

---

14 www.reggiadicaserta.beniculturali.it/

in the Introduction, Dutch people knew how to enjoy life. They headed to Vondelpark (a gorgeous park in Amsterdam) for wine and a picnic after work every time the sun would shine; they took a day off on the rare one or two days when the temperature hit 25-30º C to go to the beach or to go ice-skating on the frozen canals in the winter when the temperature dropped below -10º C. Even the top management left the office by 5:30 p.m. to get home on time for dinner with their family, and then they worked from home after the kids were asleep.

Rosaria had found a place where people didn't see life as a sacrifice. Instead, they actively pursued ways to maximize their happiness, and public administration was well-functioning and continually concerned with improving infrastructures and rules so that citizens' lives could be more enjoyable. She decided to make this country her new home and has been living there since 2002.

Since graduating with a thesis in Customer Experience (CX) in 2002, Rosaria has been a CX believer and doer. She focused on improving Customer Experience and pursuing "customer-driven growth" using NPS (Net Promoter Score) and VoC (Voice of Customer) as drivers for change. Although the projects she worked on resulted in higher revenue, loyalty, and word of mouth, and even lower costs, ultimately driving profits and business growth, she felt something was missing.

Customer-driven growth was no longer enough and, in some cases, was even misleading. Like in the case of management approaches that suggest we need to create pain in experiences to maximize memorability.

PAIN? Purposely created? Really? Why? Pain most likely happens at some point in the experience anyway because no matter how well companies design, plan, and execute, hiccups will always occur. Why create "extra pain" by design?

This thinking led to the question: "In which world would I rather live? One of pain or one of happiness?"

And as Rosaria kept pondering on this question, she gained clarity on her own WHY and became conscious about why she had chosen the field of customer experience and why she was so passionate about it. She wanted to bring **more happiness into the world, one interaction at the time**. And her chosen "change playground" was the interactions customers have with companies.

As Rosaria describes in her TEDx[15] "*Happiness-Driven-Growth: a new life-enriching business model,*" her dream is to live in a world which is:

- *Human-Centered*: business models see "companies, employees and customers" as human beings with a common shared goal: a peaceful, sustainable, healthy, and happy life.
- *Happiness-Contributing*: companies design and deliver meaningful and life-enriching products, services, and experiences for customers, enabling and empowering their employees to make a difference in peoples' lives.

She thought: since we are all on the same journey, why not make this journey as extraordinary as we can for each other? So, she started thinking about a new business model: **Happiness Driven Growth.**

Rosaria began by adding another element to Gandhi's quote, "*Happiness is when what you think, what you say, and what you do are in harmony.*" Here's her definition: "*Happiness is when what you*

15 www.wownow.eu/tedx

think, what you say, what you do, what you FEEL and WHAT YOU EXPERIENCE are in harmony."

Photo credit: Rosaria Cirillo Louwman

In this photo from May 2015, Rosaria's son is having the time of his life during their first family cruise. For him, a week of pure happiness. For Rosaria? A week of anxiety worrying about never losing sight of her two kids, considering how easily they could slip between the railings.

And a week of feeling betrayed, because when she booked the cruise, she very explicitly asked whether any adjustments had been made to these wide-open railings, having found them already terrifying seven years earlier during her honeymoon. A happy customer experience was not delivered when one was not only anticipated but expected.

Have you ever found yourself looking forward to an experience only to be disappointed by the company delivery of that experience?

Anyone can quickly point out a memory of a time they were very much looking forward to an experience only to be disappointed by the company delivery of that experience. However, nearly all the research on happiness concerns the responsibility of the individual or the government, instead of the responsibility of the company. While Rosaria strongly belicves that happiness comes from within (more about that in chapter 2), she also believes that companies have the ability, and even the responsibility, to create happiness too. After all, companies are just aggregations of people pursuing together a common goal.

Going to the supermarket, taking a train, purchasing something online, changing a subscription, and going on a cruise are all interactions with a "company" and with the people working for these companies. And what is that interaction like?

Take a moment to think about your last week and the most significant interaction you had with a company—whether it required interaction with a person or not. How did it make you FEEL (irritated, frustrated, sad, happy, delighted)? What was the consequence of this interaction? Did you complete the purchase? Did you decide never to buy from this company again? Did you tell someone or many people about the experience? What impact did this interaction have on the rest of your day? Did it make your day, or did it frustrate you?

Interactions with "companies" represent a crucial part of our daily interactions. They take up our time and generate emotions in us, ultimately influencing our happiness. When these interactions are positive, we are happy, the employees we interact with are happy, and we both start a *ripple effect of happiness* in the interactions that follow.

Unfortunately, we are so used to having mediocre interactions that we lack conscious awareness of the impact these interactions have on our time, on our happiness, and—business alert—on our subconscious purchase choices. By delivering mediocre interactions, we are missing out both on economic growth and on a better life.

Companies can deliver products and services that **empower customers to have a more meaningful and less stressful life**. They can design and deliver remarkable customer experiences that enrich peoples' lives, and they can enable human-to-human interactions that are fulfilling for both parties involved. And when they accomplish this, customers buy from them over and over again, because customers want to feel happy over and over again. And their employees are happy, feel fulfilled, and stay with these companies.

The most innovative companies are designing and delivering experiences that truly enrich lives and contribute to happiness. Zappos has made "delivering happiness" their mission, and profitability has followed. More companies are trying to get there, but they are stuck in matrices and business models that haven't stepped up yet. They can learn from the trailblazers who are already putting happiness at the center.

That is why, in 2017, Rosaria decided to start collecting systematically more examples of companies that are contributing to happiness. That's when Stan reached out to her to ask for examples of Pink Goldfish. It was just like the perfect spark at the ideal time. Rosaria reached out to Stan to propose a *Yellow Goldfish* book, and Stan immediately agreed.

This book is the result of collecting and analyzing nearly 300 cases of *Yellow Goldfish* and identifying the common threads. We hope that it can help more companies understand WHY happiness in business matters, WHAT they can do to contribute to happiness, and HOW to do so.

WHY CONTRIBUTE TO HAPPINESS

We have defined a ***Yellow Goldfish*** as anytime a business does a little extra to **contribute** to the happiness of its customers, employees, or community and society. We have identified nine paths – or ***Yellow Factor*** – that we can follow both to contribute to our own happiness and to **increase** happiness in business to delight the customer and to drive growth, productivity, and prosperity. Contributing is a keyword for us. Here's why.

1. "Happier" is a better goal than "Happy."

We believe in the approach of Tal Ben-Shahar. According to Ben-Shahar, "Am I happy?" is a closed question that suggests either you are happy, or you are not. With this question, happiness is a binary happy—unhappy with a presumed finite point that, when reached, signifies the termination of the pursuit. This point, however, does not exist, and clinging to the belief that it does will lead to dissatisfaction and frustration. We can always be happier; no person experiences happiness all the time. The better question to ask is, "How can I become happier?"[16] and "What contributes to my happiness?"

As a corollary to Ben-Shahar's question, we want to address the matter: "*How can organizations contribute more to the happiness of others—employees, customers, and society—and by doing so drive growth, prosperity, productivity, and profits*?"

2. Happiness is unlimited. We make more of it when we make others happier.

Summarizing their research on goals and happiness, Kennon Sheldon and his colleagues suggest that the pursuit of goals involving growth,

---

16 *Happier* by Tal Ben-Shahar

connection, and contribution can lead to greater well-being than goals involving money, beauty, and popularity.[17]

In *10 Keys to Happier Living,* Vanessa King's *GREAT DREAM* framework starts with **G** for **Giving.** She shares that research proves the virtuous circle of the science of giving: helping others can make us happier and happier people tend to help others more.

When companies create opportunities and potential for reciprocal happiness, and by doing so, contribute to employee, customer, and societal happiness, the natural result is growth, productivity, and prosperity.

WHY HAPPINESS IN BUSINESS

Happiness is becoming the new **competitive advantage.** Happy customers and happy employees drive **healthy growth**—even in times of crisis. Why? Happiness matters in business along three dimensions:

1. **Employees:** Happy employees have the highest return on investment (ROI) because they:

- Are more productive, creative, and innovative.
- Buy their company's products or services.
- Have lower sickness, absenteeism, and turnover rates—thereby reducing bottom-line expenses.
- Advocate for and praise the company to friends and family.
- Provide valuable feedback for improvement because they care more about their company.

---

17 *Happier* by Tal Ben-Shahar

- Deliver the best service to customers because they are happy themselves.

2. **Customers**: Happy Customers are the most profitable because they:

- Renew/repurchase and remain customers over the long term.
- Buy more and are willing to pay a premium price.
- Are more likely to forgive an experience hiccup and have a lower cost to serve.
- Promote the brand to friends and family.[18]
- Give you their most valuable asset—TIME—by providing valuable feedback for improvement, writing reviews, and engaging in your communities and forums with useful content and support for other customers.
- Live longer and are more successful: they thrive, and they buy more/longer (whether experiences, products, or services); hence they ultimately have higher Lifetime Customer Value.

3. **Society/Community: Happy citizens bring substantial benefits for society as a whole.**

The article "*Happiness and Psychological Well-Being: Building Human Capital to Benefit Individuals and Society*" on *The Solutions Journal* summaries well all the benefits.[19] Happy citizens:

- are healthy people, live longer, and enjoy a higher quality of life.

---

18 See the Forrester report "How Firms Help Employees Evoke Emotions That Deepen Customer Loyalty"
19 Source: https://www.thesolutionsjournal.com/article/happiness-and-psychological-well-being-building-human-capital-to-benefit-individuals-and-society

- Function at a higher level, utilizing their strengths, skills, and abilities to contribute to their well-being as well as that of others and society.
- Are more likely to be compassionate and, therefore, to contribute to the moral fiber of society in diversely beneficial ways.
- Are less prone to experience depression. When they do, happy citizens tend to manage it better and more quickly. They are less likely to experience anxiety, stress, or anger. As a result, happy people engage in fewer acts of violence or antisocial behaviors.
- Enjoy healthier and more-lasting relationships, thus facilitating society's social capital.

Overall, happy people contribute to society in economic, social, moral, spiritual, and psychological terms. Compared to unhappy or depressed people, the happier ones engage in fewer acts of violence. They are less of a burden to health services, social welfare agencies, and police and justice systems, and so are less of a burden to the economy. Building higher levels of individual happiness leads to the healthy, happy functioning of society as a whole.[20]

Happiness ultimately impacts your company's bottom line. How?

There are two fundamental ways happiness matters and impacts your **revenue** from the customer's point of view:

- How customers **experience** (*experiencing self*[21]) and **choose**. Emotions drive customers' immediate (purchase) decisions and what they share on social media. For decades, economists and

---

20 Additional information about these benefits and links to researches can be found on The Guardian https://www.theguardian.com/lifeandstyle/2014/nov/03/why-does-happiness-matter
21 Thinking, Fast and Slow, Daniel Kahneman

marketers assumed that our rational brain guided our purchases, but neuroscience has proven that we first make decisions emotionally and then justify them rationally. Similarly, most ratings and reviews, and social media sharing about companies, are driven by emotions, often taking place while the event is still happening (for example, while waiting in a queue or being on hold during a conversation). Forrester's CX Index shows that emotion is the strongest driver of loyalty and growth[22]. And of our feelings, happiness is the most critical driver of decisions.

- How customers **remember** (*remembering self*). Emotional events are remembered more clearly, accurately, and for more extended periods of time than neutral events[23]. Emotions are the gateway to a customer's long-term memory and hence influence what they remember. Retention, enrichment, and advocacy are influenced by what the customer remembers about the experience. Getting the key to the customer's heart (hence to long term memory) is the equivalent of getting the key to their wallet (and safe).

In 2016, Candace Payne's Happiest Chewbacca video went viral because of how quickly and easily everyone could relate to her emotion, generating the fastest sold-out Chewbacca mask ever and millions of views for KOHL's quick reaction video.[24]

While on the customer's side, emotions impact **your revenue**; on the employee's side, emotions impact **your costs**:

- **Unpleasant emotions increase sickness and absenteeism rates.** While this applies to all employees, contact center employees

---

22 See the Forrester report "Brief: Managing The Emotional Impact Of Your Customer's Experience"
23 www.ncbi.nlm.nih.gov/pmc/articles/PMC5573739/
24 www.wownow.eu/happiest-chewbacca-mom-story/

report high levels of stress due to the non-stop pressure to answer and resolve calls quickly—all while understanding customer needs and emotions and responding with effective solutions. They also have compassion fatigue. The resulting high sickness and absenteeism rates increase pressure on remaining employees, creating an endless vicious circle.

- **Psychologically healthy workplaces retain employees**. The American Psychological Association found that these workplaces have 21 percent lower turnover than the U.S. average, as well as 21 percent higher employee job satisfaction,[25] thus reducing costly hiring and training expenses.

Now let's take a look at why chemicals and needs matter to Happiness.

25 www.td.org/insights/cementing-happiness-leading-a-transformation-at-cemex

CHAPTER 2

WHY CHEMICALS AND NEEDS MATTER TO HAPPINESS

"Just like you can't look directly into the sun, you don't want to directly pursue happiness, as there's a happiness paradox; people who pursue happiness are often more depressed! The solution? Focus on attaining wholeness by cultivating wellbeing in these areas: spiritual, physical, intellectual, relational, and emotional, otherwise known as S.P.I.R.E."

– Tal Ben-Shahar

Bridging from psychology and neuroscience to business, and taking into account the learnings from our own personal happiness journeys, we see that happiness has five key aspects:

- It is the result of **chemical** reactions happening in our body.
- It is an **emotion** triggered as response to our needs and whether they are met, exceeded or unmet.
- It is a **feeling** triggered by our five senses.
- It is a **neural pathway** (like a brain muscle) that we can develop and keep active through continuous practice.
- It is an **attitude** and **way of living**, a path rather than a destination.

In this book we are going to focus on first three aspects of happiness.

THE CHEMICALS OF HAPPINESS

Life in the human body is designed to be a blissful experience. Our evolutionary biology ensures that everything necessary for our survival makes us feel good. Our brain has a wellspring of self-produced neurochemicals that turn the pursuits and struggles of life into pleasure and make us feel happy when we achieve them.[26]

Happiness comes from specific brain chemicals that evolved to do a job, not to flow all the time for no reason. When we understand their respective roles, we can find healthy new ways to stimulate them. We will look at six brain molecules linked to happiness to lay the

---

26 The Neurochemicals of Happiness, Christopher Bergland, extract from *The Athlete's Way*

foundations about **why they matter for customer and employee happiness**. We have summarized from multiples sources the most practical and straightforward descriptions of what these neurochemicals are and why they matter. Primary sources used for this part are *The Athlete's Way,* by Christopher Bergland and *A Brief History of Everything Neurochemical,* by Loretta G. Breuning, Ph.D.

In the WHAT we will cover simple ways you can apply to trigger the release of these molecules in your daily life and business to grow employee, customer, and societal happiness.

Now let's look at six significant chemicals that influence our emotions:

1. Dopamine "The Reward Molecule" or "The Molecule of Happiness"

Dopamine is responsible for reward-driven behavior and pleasure-seeking. It energizes the brain; enables us to stay focused, energized, and motivated; reduces procrastination, and allows us to feel enjoyment from the world around us.

Dopamine also affects memory, learning processes, and how we retain information. It is also the central chemical in your brain that regulates how you perceive and experience pleasure. This neurotransmitter is released during pleasurable moments or situations, which causes a person to seek out a desirable activity over and over again.[27]

Dopamine energizes you when you find a new way to meet a need. It's the brain's signal that a reward is at hand. The great feeling motivates the body to invest effort in pursuit.

Dopamine is triggered by things that promote survival in the state of nature (food, mating opportunity), and anything associated with the

27 www.blog.cognifit.com/functions-of-dopamine-serve-you/

rewards you've experienced before. Neurons connect when dopamine surges, which wires you to expect a reward in similar settings. These connections trigger a good feeling with each step closer to a prize. This mechanism motivates us to do what it takes to meet our needs.[28]

How you can leverage Dopamine in business: Create customer anticipation of the experience, add "reward" touchpoints, engage with celebrations, or other ways to recall experiences to strengthen emotional memories. Enrich journey maps to capture expectations and enlist ways to embed anticipation[29] and to increase positive memories of customer experience key moments (beginning, peak, and end). Regularly set goals that customers or employees can achieve and celebrate their achievement. Increase memorability by presenting content in a way that is new, exciting, and rewarding. Meet and exceed fulfilling universal human needs, to which we have dedicated the entire WHAT section.

2. Oxytocin: "The Bonding Molecule"

Oxytocin is directly linked to human bonding and increasing social trust and loyalty. It is sometimes called the "trust hormone." We can relax and lower our guard in the presence of trusted others. Touch and trust go together because those close enough to touch you are close enough to hurt you. In a cyber-world, where we are often "alone together" on our digital devices, it is more important than ever to maintain face-to face intimate human bonds and "tribal" connections within our community.

---

28 A Brief History of Everything Neurochemical, by Loretta G. Breuning, Ph. D www.InnerMammalInstitute.org
29 Source: Forrester Report "The Dawn Of Anticipatory CX. Anticipation Is The Missing Link In Staying Ahead Of Rising Expectations", by Ryan Hart and James L. McQuivey

You can get your fix anywhere and at any time. All you need to do is simply hug someone or shake hands. The simple act of bodily contact will cause your brain to release low levels of oxytocin—both in yourself and in the one you're touching. It's a near-instantaneous way to establish trust. Oxytocin levels also can rise when we receive a gift or when we perform together, like, for example, singing in a choir.

How you can leverage Oxytocin in business: Give your customers some love; show them you really care. Greet your customers warmly. When appropriate, add a handshake to your greeting or a warm smile to activate a mirror response. Working out at a gym, in a group environment, or having a jogging buddy is a great way to sustain human bonds and release oxytocin. Create a singing choir or perform other activities together as a team.

Coronavirus spreading in early 2020 has taken a massive toll on many oxytocin-giving practices, like handshaking or choirs. As an alternative, you can increase the number of hugs within your family, of gifts exchange or participation in virtual sing-alongs with colleagues and clients, of massages sessions bookings for yourself.

3. Serotonin: "The Confidence Molecule"

Serotonin is one of the relaxing chemicals in the brain, and it impacts how we feel about ourselves and the world. Being able to say, "I did it!" produces a feedback loop that reinforces behaviors that build self-esteem, reduce insecurity, and create an upward spiral of serotonin.[30] A weird thing about serotonin is that you make more of it while you're happy and less of it while you're sad—when you would need it most. This dynamic is why, like Gretchen Rubin explains in her book *The Happiness Project*, acting happy, even if you are not, will

---

30 The Neurochemicals of Happiness, Christopher Bergland, extract from The Athlete's Way

eventually start making you happy. Interestingly, research shows that thinking of past happy times creates just as much serotonin as being in a present happy moment.

Serotonin also increases when you gain a social advantage. Mammals compare themselves to others to avoid conflict. They make careful decisions about when to assert and when to defer. Serotonin is released when a mammal sees itself in the one-up position.[31]

This mechanism is the reason why some people may actively pursue power and dominance and why power becomes addictive. Power can be some people's path to happiness, even though one that happens at the cost of other's happiness as opposed to the win-win Happiness Driven Growth we are emphasizing in our book.

By inducing our brain to release and increase serotonin, and other chemicals of happiness, in ways that are beneficial for each other, we can achieve broader world happiness and reduce power struggles, wars, and many other forms of social disparity.

How you can leverage Serotonin in business: Create and do things that reinforce a sense of purpose, meaning, and accomplishment, and that build self-esteem (both in your customers and employees) by allowing them to say "yes, I did it." Allow nap-time and have nap rooms in the office; enable and stimulate employees to have lunch or coffee outside and go for a walking meeting so that they can have at least 20 minutes of sun a day; offer on-site massages; take pictures of happy moments during company off-sites and hang them around the office; take photos of customers during happy moments (or enable/nudge customers to do so) and send these pictures as a reminder few weeks after the experience or at its anniversary. Facebook is using this approach with their videos celebrating

---

31 www.InnerMammalInstitute.org

anniversaries or special moments and with daily Memories, formerly OTD (On This Day).

4. Endorphin: "The Pain-Killing Molecule"

The body produces endorphins in response to pain, excitement, and exercise. Along with regular exercise, laughter is one of the easiest ways to induce endorphin release. Even the anticipation and expectation of laugher, e.g., attending a comedy show, increases levels of endorphins. The smell of vanilla, lavender, chocolate, and spicy foods have been linked with the production of endorphins.

How you can leverage Endorphins in business: Have a gym at the office, participate as a company in running or other sports competitions, offer acupuncture on-site for your employees. Take your sense of humor to work, forward that funny email, find things to laugh about during the day. Use scented oils in your workplace and offer dark chocolate that not only causes the release of endorphins but serotonin as well.

5. GABA: "The Anti-Anxiety Molecule"

GABA gives the ability to relax because it creates a sense of calmness by slowing down the firing of neurons and allowing them time to recover. GABA relieves anxiety and reduces stress.

How you can leverage GABA in business: Promote meditation practice. Offer yoga classes or chair massages for employees. Provide a quiet, relax room. San Francisco's airport has a dedicated yoga room that is often referenced on social media as the distinctive mark of this airport. The newly rebuilt hospital in Zaandam in the Netherlands has a "Stilte room" ("Calmness room") to take a moment of peace and reflection, regardless of culture or religion.

6. Adrenaline: "The Energy Molecule"

Adrenaline plays a significant role in the fight or flight mechanism. It creates a surge in energy and makes you feel alive. It can be an antidote for boredom, malaise, and stagnation. Taking risks and doing scary things that force you out of your comfort zone is key to maximizing your human potential.

How you can leverage Adrenaline in business: Keep customer energy and interest high by keeping things new and exciting. For employees, consider outdoor activities for your off-sites: rafting, kart racing, or kart-surfing on the Dutch beaches, obstacle courses. Set-up mini competitions with deadlines and fun rewards.

FINAL THOUGHTS ON THE CHEMICALS OF HAPPINESS

These are the most simplified notions relevant to better understanding yourself, your employees, and your customers. Still, brain science is a triad of **electrical** (brain waves), **architectural** (brain structures), and **chemical** (neurochemicals) components working in concert to create a state of mind. While we won't go further into these details, here are three more things we have to consider in our search of creating happiness in business[32]:

a. Habituation

---

32 A Brief History of Everything Neurochemical based on the book *Habits of a Happy Brain. Retrain Your Brain to Boost Your Serotonin, Dopamine, Oxytocin and Endorphin Levels* by Loretta Graziano Breuning, PhD www.InnerMammalInstitute.org

The brain saves its happy chemicals for new rewards and habituates quickly to old rewards. For this reason, we're often disappointed by the same old thing, and we're always seeking something new.

b. Cortisol

Cortisol commands attention when a threat is perceived (internal or external). Disappointment triggers cortisol, alerting that expectations are not met, so the brain stops investing energy in an unrewarding pursuit.

c. Mirror Neurons

When you see someone enjoy something, mirror neurons respond as if you are having the experience yourself.

How you can leverage these elements in business:

- Keep habituation low by doing unexpected things for a limited time; make new offers, add unique benefits.
- Reduce cortisol production by giving your customers and employees clear communication about expectations and by exceeding expectations (remember you can never meet expectations—you either exceed them or you fall short and trigger cortisol).
- Use the power of mirror neurons to spread positivity and multiply happiness. We will cover more on this in the chapter about the final S (Smile) of Happiness.

In short: We try to stimulate good feelings in ways that worked before. Because these chemicals are released in short spurts, they are soon metabolized. We always have to do more to get more. Our neurochemical operating system evolved to motivate survival behavior. It rewards us for steps toward meeting our needs.[33]

Use the above list of neurochemicals and the Types we cover in the WHAT as a checklist to take inventory of your business and personal daily habits and to contribute to the best balance possible. Four chemicals have the most impact on this balance and are the **unmissable DOSE of happiness that you need to inject in your business**:

- **D**opamine is your brain's signal that a reward is at hand. The joyful, excited feeling is released when you approach something that meets an unmet need.
- **O**xytocin is the good feeling of social trust. It's released when you find the safety of social support, when you hug someone, or where there is a useful touchpoint.
- **S**erotonin is calm confidence in your ability. It's released when you pursue things that reinforce a sense of purpose, meaning, and accomplishment, and when you relax or think of happy memories.
- **E**ndorphin is released when you exercise and when you laugh.

Experiences that release the DOSE[34] neurochemicals make us happy, and that makes us want more of the same. For this reason, we ultimately purchase what makes us HAPPY (or we expect it will) from people we TRUST.

Design and deliver your experiences in a way that provides customers and employees a high DOSE of happiness.

---

33 Source: Stimulate Your Dopamine, Serotonin, and Oxytocin - by Loretta G. Breuning, PhD

34 Acronyms Source: www.technologyadvice.com/blog/information-technology/activate-chemicals-gamify-happiness-nicole-lazzaro/

Now let's look at why human NEEDS matter.

THE LINK BETWEEN NEEDS AND EMOTIONS

Happiness is also an emotion that people feel in response to their needs and whether these are unmet, met, or exceeded. A clear understanding of people's needs is foundational to be able to understand and influence the emotions a customer is feeling.

For over 15 years, during her work as Business Improvement Manager and Customer Experience manager first and Customer Experience Consultant later, Rosaria gathered and analyzed information from customer satisfaction (CSAT) and Net Promoters Score (NPS) survey projects run for different companies across multiple touchpoints and industry verticals. Her analysis determined that an adapted version of Maslow's hierarchy of needs can be applied. She found there was a clear correlation between the CSAT/NPS Scores and which level of needs the customer felt was fulfilled during the interaction or by the company relationship overall.[35] Since 2016, Rosaria has added the emotions to the model, as we can see in this figure.[36]

35 www.wownow.eu/net-promoter-score-explained-with-maslow-needs-hierarchy/
36 www.wownow.eu/customer-understanding/

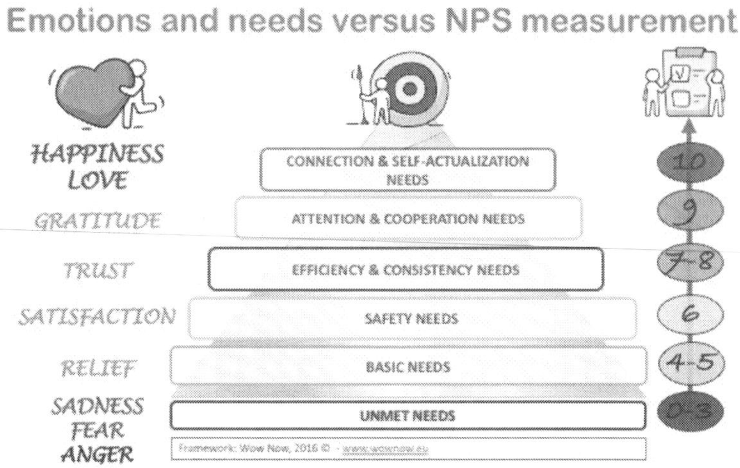

Figure 3. Correlation between NPS score versus Consumer's hierarchy of needs in Customer Service. Source: Rosaria Cirillo, Wow Now

Emotions have a direct correlation with needs—a straightforward one.

As Marshall Rosenberg explains in his book *Nonviolent Communication: A Language of Life*, there are no positive or negative emotions, but only emotions we feel when our needs are met and when our needs are not met. When our needs are not met, we feel anger, frustration, disappointment, or sadness. When our needs are met, we feel relieved, satisfied, trusting, appreciative, or happy (Rosenberg, 2005). In the cruise example shared earlier, Rosaria didn't get her safety needs met, and that limited her overall happiness.

Rosaria has observed that when this framework (see figure above) is used to identify, prioritize, and execute actions, companies achieved higher customer satisfaction, more promoters, lower contact center costs, and even higher employee retention within three to six months. Why? Because the steps taken moved both employees and customers up the pyramid of needs and emotions.

Customer happiness and process efficiency improved because actions taken addressed root causes of identified failures and provided better responses to each level of needs.

Employee happiness improved because customer comments gave them visibility on the impact they had on customer lives. The comments gave them praise for their work, and made them feel they contributed to someone's happiness. Simple comments like "a special thanks to Lotte, she really made my day with her help and her smiling voice" made Lotte truly happy and motivated to do her work.

Happiness happens at the top of the pyramid. The rest is functional and is about success and meeting needs. The peak of the pyramid and above is about desires, unrecognized needs, collective growth, and purpose. By focusing on the top of the pyramid, we both contribute to everyone's happiness, and we drive business growth.

The Etymology of "emotion."

The word ***emotion*** comes from the Greek word *emotere,* which means "*energy in motion.*" The roots for *motion* and *emotion* are virtually identical. *Movere*, from the Latin, means to move. *Exmovere* or *emovere* means to move out, hence to excite. So, taking action stirs up something and moves something inside of us. **Emotions have the purpose of getting us in motion.** Emotions move us away from a desireless state, motivating us to act.

Because dopamine is the chemical most impacting our happiness and because it's released when we approach something that meets a need, it seems only too evident and consequent that when we meet our needs, we feel happy.

Pursuing things and experiences that meet our needs, we trigger the release of Dopamine, which is both our "reward molecule" and the chemical that allows us to think more clearly, make decisions, and feel better about life overall; therefore, we activate the best virtuous circle possible.

As Tal Ben-Shahar describes in his book *Happier*, we don't just want to feel the emotions, we also want the **cause of the feeling to be meaningful**. We want to know that the actions that have given us good emotions have an actual effect on the world.

For this reason, we need to look at Happiness not only as chemistry (or else we could just take a pill of DOSE) but also as the feeling we feel when our highest needs (the top of Maslow's pyramid) are met and exceeded, and when we live our experiences with all the five senses.

We will talk more about this in Chapter 5, *Uncovering Happiness*. First, a fun test for you to check your chemical balance before we move on to explore the metaphors behind the Yellow Goldfish.

FOR FUN: TEST YOUR CHEMICALS BALANCE[37]

If you want to know what neurotransmitter you may be low in, take this brief four-question quiz. It was designed to check which chemicals may impact your weight; hence it doesn't include all the six chemicals of happiness. Choose the one letter in each question that best describes you. If none represents you, then leave the question blank. If more than one describes you, choose them all.

1. I crave:

a. I love chocolate and/or coffee and/or sugar.

b. I love fatty things like cream cheese, guacamole, and chocolate mousse.

c. I love bread, pasta, and salty snacks.

d. I don't care what it is. I just want enough of it to make me feel full.

2. At work or school:

a. I find it challenging to stay focused, have drops in energy, and procrastinate.

b. I can never remember what I just did, I may have to redial the phone multiple times, and I can be slow to catch on.

c. People can easily annoy me, I usually trust my ideas over others, and I sometimes feel others are out to get me.

d. I get anxious and worry about every little thing so much so that I sometimes have trouble getting things done.

---

37 Source: "Is Your Brain Making You Fat?" /www.metaboliceffect.com/is-your-brain-making-you-fat/

3. Exercise makes me feel:

a. More energized and powerful.

b. Smarter and more creative.

c. Happier and more attractive.

d. Calmer with fewer worries.

4. If I feel depressed, it is most likely to be:

a. A feeling of frustration that I can't ever stick to a plan or schedule or fulfill promises to myself.

b. A feeling of mental slowness, mental frustration, or feelings that I am just not as smart as others.

c. I am just sad without any good reason. I often wish I looked different or was someone sexier, smarter, and more likable.

d. An anxious worrying type depression. Anxiety rather than depression more defines me.

Now total up your answers. If any letter was chosen two or more times, then there is a good chance you have a deficiency in that neurotransmitter. Keep in mind you can often have more than one deficiency and also may have none.

Here are how the letters break down.

a. Dopamine
b. Acetylcholine (the chemical that motor neurons of the nervous system release to activate muscles)[38]
c. Serotonin
d. GABA

Obviously, this is a simplified questionnaire with weaknesses because of its subjective nature. Other than checking how you are doing for the fun of it, the critical thing to understand is that the brain chemicals have a direct impact on mood, cravings, motivation, hunger, energy, focus, self-esteem, problem-solving, sleep, and more. Those in the alternative medicine community often refer to these chemicals as the "molecules of emotion," precisely because they impact so much of what we do, who we are, and how we feel.

Now that you know which chemicals you crave the most, you are ready to move to the WHAT part where you will learn how you can increase each of these chemicals in business. First, though, let's look at why yellow and why goldfish behind the metaphor of Yellow Goldfish.

---

38 www.en.wikipedia.org/wiki/Acetylcholine

CHAPTER 3

WHY A GOLDFISH & A SUNFLOWER?

"Big doors swing on little hinges"

- W. Clement Stone

WHY A GOLDFISH

BY STAN PHELPS

The origin of the goldfish dates back to 2009. It has become a signature part of my book series. *Yellow Goldfish* is the seventh color in the series. The goldfish represents something small, but despite its size, something with the ability to make a big difference.

The first part of the inspiration for the goldfish came from Kimpton Hotels. The boutique hotel chain introduced something new in 2001. The Kimpton Hotel Monaco began to offer travelers the opportunity to adopt a temporary travel companion for their stay. Perhaps you are traveling on business and getting a little lonely. Or maybe you are with the family and missing your family pet. Kimpton to the rescue; they will give you a goldfish for your stay. They call the program Guppy Love.

"The 'Guppy Love' program is a fun extension of our pet-friendly nature as well as our emphasis on indulging the senses to heighten the travel experience," says Steve Pinetti, Senior Vice President of Sales & Marketing for Kimpton Hotels and Restaurants, of which Hotel Monaco is part of their premier collection. "Everything about Hotel Monaco appeals directly to the senses, and 'Guppy Love' offers one more unique way to relax, indulge and promote the health of mind, body, and spirit in our home-away-from-home atmosphere."

The second part of our goldfish inspiration came from the unusual growth of a goldfish. The average common goldfish is between three to four inches in length (ten centimeters), yet the largest in the world is almost six times that size! For comparison, imagine walking down the street and bumping into someone who's three stories tall.

How can there be such a disparity between regular goldfish and their monster cousins? Well, it turns out that five factors determine the growth of the goldfish. Just like goldfish, not all businesses grow equally, and we believe that the growth of a product or service faces the same five factors that affect the growth of a goldfish.

#1. SIZE OF THE ENVIRONMENT = THE MARKET

GROWTH FACTOR: The size of the bowl or pond.

IMPACT: Direct correlation. The larger the bowl or pond, the more giant the goldfish can grow. Similarly, the smaller the market in business, the lesser the growth potential.

#2. NUMBER OF OTHER GOLDFISH IN THE BOWL OR POND = COMPETITION

GROWTH FACTOR: The number of goldfish in the same bowl or pond.

IMPACT: Inverse correlation. The more goldfish, the less growth. Similarly, the less competition in business, the more growth opportunity exists.

#3. THE QUALITY OF THE WATER = THE ECONOMY

GROWTH FACTOR: The clarity and amount of nutrients in the water.

IMPACT: Direct correlation. The better the quality, the more significant the growth. Similarly, the weaker the economy or capital markets in business, the more difficult it is to grow.

FACT

A malnourished goldfish in a crowded, cloudy environment may only grow to two inches (five centimeters).

#4. THE FIRST 120 DAYS OF LIFE = START-UP PHASE OR A NEW PRODUCT LAUNCH

GROWTH FACTOR: The nourishment and treatment received as a fry (baby goldfish).

IMPACT: Direct correlation. The lower the quality of the food, water, and treatment, the more the goldfish will be stunted for future growth. Similarly, in business, the more robust the leadership and capital for a start-up, the better the growth.

#5. GENETIC MAKEUP = DIFFERENTIATION

GROWTH FACTOR: The genetic makeup of the goldfish.

IMPACT: Direct correlation. The weaker the genes or the less differentiated, the less the goldfish can grow. Similarly, in business, the more differentiated the product or service from the competition, the better the chance for growth.

> FACT
>
> The current Guinness World Record holder for the largest goldfish hailed from the Netherlands at a lengthy 19 inches (50 centimeters). To put that in perspective, that's about the size of the average domesticated house cat.

WHICH OF THE FIVE FACTORS CAN YOU CONTROL?

Let's assume you have an existing product or service and have been in business for more than four months. Do you have any control over the market, your competition, or the economy? NO, NO, and NO.

The only thing you have control over is your business's genetic makeup or how you differentiate your product or service. In goldfish terms, how do you stand out in a sea of sameness?

We believe that **happiness can drive differentiation**.

WHY A SUNFLOWER

BY ROSARIA CIRILLO

We chose the sunflower as representation of the What (each petal representing an element of Happiness, aka a *Yellow Factor*) and the How (for each stage of *Growth*), both covered in section II and III.

The inspiration for the sunflower comes from three elements:

- Sunflowers' growth
- Seeds
- Sun

#1. **Sunflowers' growth** – Most people are in owe when looking at sunflower fields in full blossom. They generally convey happiness both because of their beauty and of their yellow color, which we explain in the next chapter. They symbolize worship and faithfulness in various religions because of their resemblance to the sun, which is associated with spiritual knowledge and the desire to seek light and truth. They are often given on 3rd year wedding anniversaries as signs of admiration, strength, zest for living, loyalty, faith, fertility. And they blossom in the summer, the season in which we tend to feel happier.

As you will read in chapter 11 (Nature) and 23 (Lagniappe: Sunflowers), while Stan and I were writing *Yellow Goldfish*, in April 2018 I seeded sunflowers in my garden for the first time, and together with kids we enjoyed watching their growth and awing at the different height they reached.

In March 2019, the kids came back home from school with a lovely project: they had received a sunflowers' seeds bag and a "growth journal" with the task to plant the seeds in a transparent container & monitor the growth day by day across the entire life cycle of the sunflower. We planted the seeds on a sunshining afternoon, the 20 of

March, which is actually *International Day of Happiness*, and followed the growth very closely day by day, monitoring how many seeds actually sprouted and all possible differences between their two pots.Having planted the seeds in transparent (tomatoes) containers, allowed us to take note of many details. Over ten seeds from my son Mauro sprouted, while for Raul only four and two of them actually got broken by a book that happened to fall on them, just when they had grown into small plants of 5-10 cm. We carefully transposed the "survivors" from the small containers into the ground soil in the garden.

In July, four months later, only one of Mauro's ten plants was still growing and had already blossomed, while both the two sprouts from Raul had kept growing, one becoming over 2 meters tall!! On the 5th of July kids were also asked to bring in a picture of their sunflowers and it was remarkable to see how much difference in growth when looking at all the photos from all the kids.

The five elements that can make a difference in the growth of a goldfish (water, size of the bowl, number of fishes in the bowl, first 90 days and DNA), very much influence also the sunflowers growth & blossoming:

#1. SIZE OF THE ENVIRONMENT = THE MARKET

GROWTH FACTOR: The size of the pot or ground extension.

IMPACT: Direct correlation. The larger the pot or ground, the bigger the sunflower can grow. Similarly, the smaller the market in business, the lesser the growth potential.

#2. NUMBER OF OTHER SEEED IN THE POT OR SOIL = COMPETITION

GROWTH FACTOR: The number of seeds in the same pot or ground, and how close to each other they are planted.

IMPACT: Inverse correlation. The more seeds and the closer to each other, the less growth. Similarly, the less competition in business, the more growth opportunity exists.

#3. THE QUALITY OF THE GROUND = THE ECONOMY

GROWTH FACTOR: The quality/amount of nutrients in the ground.

IMPACT: Direct correlation. The better the quality, the more significant the growth. Similarly, the weaker the economy or capital markets in business, the more difficult it is to grow.

#4. THE FIRST 60 DAYS OF LIFE = START-UP PHASE

GROWTH FACTOR: The sun, water, nourishment and treatment received as a sprout.

IMPACT: Direct correlation. The lower the quality of the water and treatment, the worst the weather and the more snails and slugs around, the more the sunflowers will be stunted for future growth. Similarly, in business, the more robust the leadership and capital for a start-up, the better the growth.

#5. GENETIC MAKEUP = DIFFERENTIATION

GROWTH FACTOR: The genetic makeup of the seeds.

IMPACT: Direct correlation. The weaker the genes or the less differentiated, the less the sunflower can grow. Similarly, in business, the more differentiated the product, service or experience from the competition, the better the chance for growth.

WHICH OF THE FIVE FACTORS CAN YOU INFLUENCE?

Over the last few years, and even more so during the Covid pandemic in 2020 which proved how lack of Health (the first Yellow Factor) can totally impact the economy, I have come to believe that Happiness actually allows us to influence all of the five factors!

FACT

The current Guinness World Record holder for the tallest sunflower measures 9.17 m (30 ft 1 in) and was grown by Hans-Peter Schiffer in Karst, Nordrhein Westfalen, Germany, as verified on 28 August 2014.

#2. **Seeds** – Second, the seeds. Not only sunflowers' seeds are a key element for their own growth, but once the sunflower has reached its full blossoming, contributing to the happiness of anyone who looks at them, their seeds actually take on a life of their own with dozens of possible uses and further contribution to other species' growth and happiness. Just few examples:

- They are a source of food for birds and animals.
- They are edible for us too. They can be eaten raw, cooked, roasted or dried. They are a popular, nutritious snack containing a good source of protein, vitamins A, B, and E, calcium, nitrogen and iron.
- They can be used to make sunflower oil, a popular vegetable oil known for its light color, mild flavor, low levels of saturated fats and ability to withstand high cooking temperatures.

#3. **Sun** – Finally, the sun.

Sunflowers get energy through photosynthesis. The bud (the first flower head sunflower matures around 35 to 65 days after seeding) tries to get all the hours of sunlight possible in order to gain energy to develop and enlarge; it does this by following the sun, a fascinating phenomenon called heliotropism, an inbuilt mechanism which has evolved over thousands of generation of sunflowers in order to take full advantage of natural light for photosynthesis. The daily process of tracking the sun only goes on as long as the sunflower is in the bud and young flower head stage. Once the full flower emerges, the sunflower head stops following the sun and stations itself by facing East all the time, so that it can focus all its attention on growing as a big bloom and attracting pollinators. Following the sun, the plant can nourish itself, converting the sun's energy into chemicals that will make the overall plant big, strong and healthy enough to support the large flower head when it opens.

In many different faith traditions as well as in the secular world, many people are encouraged to be light to others or to bring light to others: in times of darkness we can offer hope, encouragement, kindness and compassion; in times where others are struggling we can offer a way to help them to see the good and the beautiful so they can regain their glow and shine; in times of doubts to "Be the Light" may be to offer wisdom and guidance, or just to sit with someone, and be the presence they need; in times of difficulties, we can show support and resilience to those that are feeling vulnerable; finally, at any time we can simply offer a smile and joy to someone, in random parts of our day. And most all, we can all be role model and increase overall light and energy, by turning on our own light.

One of my favorite rituals from a Leadership retreat I joined last year organized by Eva Visser Plaza, it has been to start every day, and later every meeting lead by Eva, with each participant turning on a candle repeating: "*When I turn on my light, I turn on the light in other's too*". A great reminder of the intention with which we want to live and lead our *Feminine Authentic Leadership.*

Even when companies choose other ways than happiness to differentiate themselves, every company and each of us can still have a *Yellow Factor* and **do their little extra that seeds happiness, shines sunlight and contributes to a happier, healthier world**.

Now, why the color yellow?

CHAPTER 4

WHY YELLOW?

"I have noticed that most people in this world are about as happy as they have made up their minds to be."

- attributed to Abraham Lincoln by Frank Crane

Yellow is the seventh color in the Goldfish series. So why did we choose yellow? There are a few reasons…

#1. **Primary** - First, it's because yellow is one of the three primary colors. It is the brightest and most cheerful of all the colors in the spectrum. As a color specialist and the executive director of the Pantone Color Institute, Leatrice Eiseman[39] has conducted various color word-association studies on thousands of people over the last 30 years. She has found that the first words that consistently come to mind when people see the color yellow are "warmth," "cheer," "happiness," and sometimes even "playfulness."

Why do we have these feelings? It's because we associate yellow with the sun. Interestingly, the sun is actually white. We perceive it as yellow or orange because of the higher wavelengths of these colors. Yellow is scattered less easily by Earth's atmosphere, leaving the color for us to see. Blue, on the other hand, has low wavelengths, which explains why it is strewn across the sky. According to *Empowered By Color*,[40] because yellow is the lightest hue of the spectrum, the color is uplifting and illuminating, offering hope, happiness, cheerfulness, and fun.

Tal Ben-Shahar uses the metaphor that happiness is like the white light of the sun. If you look straight into it, it's blinding, so instead of pursuing happiness directly (looking into the sun), we need to pursue happiness indirectly, focusing on things that make us happy. In business, this is the equivalent of focusing on the nine types of *Yellow Factor* we identify in Part Two of this book.

The sun represents warmth, which leads us to our next reason.

---

39 www.cnn.com/2017/06/30/health/cnn-colorscope-yellow/index.html
40 www.empower-yourself-with-color-psychology.com/color-yellow.html

#2. **Warmth** - We use yellow as a metaphor because of warmth. In our evolution as humans, we are programmed to look for warmth instinctively. As we have evolved, we developed skills integral to our survival. One talent was the ability to make judgments about our surroundings with a high degree of speed and accuracy. As we walked out of the "cave," our senses immediately jumped into survival mode. In a split second, we assessed everyone we encountered on two primary criteria:

1. Were they a threat?

2. What was their ability to carry out that threat?

Research conducted by Susan T. Fiske and Chris Malone in the book *The Human Brand* has shown that over 80 percent of our judgments are based on these two factors even today. Assigning characteristics to our perception, we can label these as warmth and competence. These perceptions don't just apply to people. We also use the same standards for products and companies. We automatically perceive and judge their behaviors on a subconscious level. Brands are people too.

According to an article in *Harvard Business Review* [41] by Amy J.C. Cuddy, Matthew Kohut, and John Neffinger,

> A growing body of research suggests that the way to influence—and to lead—is to begin with warmth. Warmth is the conduit of influence: It facilitates trust and the communication and absorption of ideas. Even a few small nonverbal signals—a nod, a smile, an open gesture—can show people that you're pleased to be in their company and attentive to their concerns. Prioritizing warmth helps you connect immediately with those around you,

41 www.hbr.org/2013/07/connect-then-lead

> demonstrating that you hear them, understand them, and can be trusted by them.

In the words of Chris Malone, perhaps the most significant takeaway is this, "Companies need to embrace significant change in the way they do business with customers, better aligning their policies, practices, and processes to reflect warmth and competence."

#3. **Follow the Ball** - The overwhelming majority of tennis balls are yellow. The color was first introduced in 1972 following research demonstrating that "optic" yellow was more visible on television. However, this is not the "Ball" that inspires our use of yellow. We were inspired by the round smiley face created by American graphic artist Harvey Ross Ball.

According to the *Smithsonian,*[42] Ball was engaged by State Mutual Life Assurance Company of Worcester, Massachusetts, to create a happy face. The goal by State Mutual, now known as Hanover Insurance, was to raise the morale of the employees. Ball's iconic graphic involved a bright yellow background, dark oval eyes, a full smile, and creases at the sides of the mouth. It took 10 minutes to create the smiley face, and Ball was paid $45 for the graphic.

Over the next fifty years, versions of the smiley face would be imprinted on more than fifty million buttons and became famous around the world. It has become an icon for happiness and is responsible for spawning the development of digital emoticons. On the Internet, the smiley has become a visual means of conveying joy. The first known mention of them on the Internet was on September 19, 1982, when Scott Fahlman from Carnegie Mellon University wrote, "I propose the following character sequence for joke markers:

---

42 www.smithsonianmag.com/arts-culture/who-really-invented-the-smiley-face-2058483/

:-). Read it sideways. Actually, it is probably more economical to mark things that are NOT jokes, given current trends. For this, use:

:-(."

Now that we've explored the meaning behind yellow and goldfish, the next part of the book will focus on the nine different types of *Yellow Factor*.

Ready to find H.A.P.P.I.N.E.S.S? Let's go...

SECTION II

THE TYPES (THE WHAT)

CHAPTER 5

UNCOVERING H.A.P.P.I.N.E.S.S.

"Happiness is when what we think, what we say, what we do, what we FEEL, and what we EXPERIENCE are in harmony"

- Rosaria Cirillo Louwman

THE INTERSECTION OF EXPERIENCE AND HAPPINESS

Happiness is a feeling, but it's also about perception. Perceptions and emotions are the cornerstones of both customer and employee experience. In the words of the late poet Maya Angelou, "I've learned that people will forget what you said, people will forget what you did, but people will never forget how you made them feel."

Let's examine customer experience (CX) and employee experience (EX) through their traditional definitions.

Customer experience is defined as "*how customers and employees perceive their interactions with the company*." Two keywords in the definition have a broader meaning and application:

- *Perception*: is how your customers think and feel about what you do.
- *Interactions*: encompass all of the experiences with your organization.

CX experts & companies like Forrester and Temkin Group believe that customers and employees perceive these interactions along three dimensions:

1. Effectiveness (how much it meets needs)

2. Easiness (how easy it is to interact)

3. Emotion (how does the interaction make them feel)

Our observations and analysis show that customers and employees perceive these interactions throughout all of their five senses with their body (sight, smell, hear, touch, and taste) and along five dimensions with their minds and hearts. In addition to the three dimensions already mentioned, these extra two play a crucial role:

4. Realization & meaning (how much the interaction fulfills desires, shared values, and a common purpose)
5. Timing of the experience (resolution speed) and of the person living the experience (during which life events is taking place)

People compare this perception with three references:

1. Expectations
2. Previous experiences (with you or with competitors)
3. Alternatives available

Together, these five dimensions, five senses and three references, determine the perceived value for money, the alignment to a person's life values, and the likelihood to repurchase or recommend a given product/company to others.

In the context of CX and EX, *happiness is what we feel when the maximum potential for the minimum effort/resources is obtained, and when as many of the five dimensions and senses as possible are orchestrated into a remarkable and memorable experience, which exceeds our three references.*

SEEKING HAPPINESS

How can you design and deliver experiences that delight customers, employees, and society overall? Our goal was to answer that question through the *Yellow Goldfish project* using the data collected from the nearly 300 companies we researched. We specifically looked for ways that brands can enhance happiness in business and for little things that can make a big difference.

In reviewing all of the companies, we began to see patterns. We noticed that brands could leverage nine different ways to drive happiness for customers, employees, and society.

As opposed to the wheel of fortune of ancient times or to the "wheel of life" of current times, we thought of introducing the "sunflower of happiness" to symbolize the nine ways to blossom towards happiness.

The nine ways make the acronym of H.A.P.P.I.N.E.S.S. and the nine petals:

H is for Health

A is for Autonomy

P is for Purpose

P is for Play

I is for Integrity

N is for Nature

E is for Empathy

S is for Simplicity

S is for Smile

Over the next nine chapters, we'll explore each type. We'll share case studies of brands that represent each element of H.A.P.P.I.N.E.S.S.

The psychology of universal human needs has been the standard and driving framework in identifying the nine ways. In each chapter, we explore the universal human needs addressed in each category, leveraging insights from Maslow's hierarchy of needs, Marshall Rosenberg's findings,[43] and other sources (mostly from Yoram Mosenzon[44] and Cara Crisler[45]).

Also, where relevant, we'll share the science and research, the chemistry, and suggest additional ways to bring each element to life in business.

Let's go. Health is the first...

Figure 4. The Sunflower of Happiness.

43 *Nonviolent Communication. A Language of Life.* by Marshall B. Rosenberg, Ph. D.
44 www.connecting2life.net/
45 www.crislercoaching.com/resources/

CHAPTER 6

HEALTH

"Our greatest happiness does not depend on the condition of life in which chance has placed us, but is always the result of a good conscience, good health, occupation, and freedom in all just pursuits."

-- Thomas Jefferson

THIS CHAPTER IN FIVE SENSES

- Waterfall
- Lavender
- Song: *Stayin 'Alive* (Bee Gees)
- Curcuma
- Water

TEDx Talk:

What if we paid Doctors to keep people healthy?

Matthias Mullenbeck

THE "H" IN H.A.P.P.I.N.E.S.S. STANDS FOR HEALTH.

It all starts with Health. Without health, we have nothing in life, and happiness is a non-starter. It's an easy concept to grasp. You need to manage your health as a fundamental need to achieve a state of wellness.

More than just wellness, health enhances productivity and happiness. Max Borges of the Max Borges Agency breaks it down further, "When you feel good physically, you feel good mentally." Borges' South Florida company does public relations for the consumer electronics industry. It offers its employees benefits such as an onsite gym, fitness classes, and reimbursement for athletic competition entry fees. "If there's a fountain of youth, it is probably physical activity. Research has shown benefits to every organ system in the body. So, the problem isn't whether it's a good idea. The problem is how to get people to do more of it,'' according to Dr. Toni Yancey.

We include under the "HEALTH" category the following universal human needs:

- Air
- Comfort
- Emotional Safety
- Exercise/Movement
- Food
- Light
- Protection
- Rest/Sleep

- Safety/Security
- Water

Let's look at six *Yellow Goldfish* we found for this Yellow Factor.

#1. GOOGLE HEALTH AND HAPPINESS

In 2011, Google was crowned the "HAPPIEST COMPANY IN AMERICA" by CareerBliss.com. The study looked at 100,000+ worker-generated reviews spanning over 10,000 companies. Scores were based on such factors as work-life balance, relationships with bosses and co-workers, compensation, growth opportunities, company culture, and the opportunity for employees to exert control over their daily workflow.

Yellow Goldfish – The Googleplex: The company takes the health of team members seriously. At the Googleplex Campus, you're sure to see the multi-colored bicycles that Googlers use to get between campus buildings and strange works of art, including a life-size Tyrannosaurus Rex skeleton. There is also a sand volleyball court and organic gardens where they grow many of the fresh vegetables used in the campus restaurant.

The GARField (Google Athletic Recreation Field) Park includes sports fields and tennis courts that are opened up to public use on nights and weekends. You can swim in one of the Googleplex lap pools. The outdoor mini-pools are like water treadmills: a strong current allows employees to swim and swim and go nowhere. Luckily, according to *How Stuff Works*, lifeguards are always on duty in case someone gets in over their head.

To cater to spiritual health, Google offers mindfulness training. The course called "Search Inside Yourself," regularly has a waitlist stretching six months. If you work at the Googleplex, you can also eat breakfast, lunch, and dinner free of charge. There are several cafés located throughout the campus, and employees can eat at any of them.

The main café is Charlie's Place. The café takes its name from Google's first lead chef, Charlie Ayers. Before creating meals for Googlers, Ayers was the chef for the Grateful Dead. Although Ayers left Google in 2005, the café still bears his name. The café has several stations, each offering different kinds of cuisine. Options range from vegetarian dishes to sushi to ethnic foods from around the world. Google's culture promotes the use of fresh, organic foods and healthy meals.

#2. HALTON HEALTHCARE AND KAILO

Employees without a sense of wellness tend to take excessive sick days and suffer from low job satisfaction. Leaders at Canada's Halton Healthcare were faced with these exact issues. They found a solution in "*Kailo*," a decidedly psycho-social framework for staff wellness that was developed at Mercy Medical Center in Northern Iowa. Kailo, an ancient word meaning *whole*, pulls into balance all aspects of health and well-being, including social, emotional, spiritual, and physical elements. "We wanted to build trust and improve relationships among employees. Kailo offered proven approaches to demonstrate respect and value for all employees regardless of their current health practices, and allowed us also to promote humor, fun, and play in the workplace," says Anna Rizzotto, Halton's Kailo Coordinator.

Yellow Goldfish - Kailo Moments: Times of caring and sharing among co-workers were dubbed "Kailo" moments. Staff embraced all the benefits of Kailo, including "Kailo- to-Go" in-services, the Kailo Treat Kart, the Kailo First Aid Basket, and the ever-popular mini-massage. According to Rizzotto, "The feel-good impact of mini-massage appears to surpass all other program offerings!"

#3. UNILEVER AND EAP

Unilever UK takes a holistic approach to health and wellbeing. They focus on the mental, physical and emotional elements of wellbeing, as well as a sense of purpose. The company offers a wide range of support from an employee assistance program (EAP) and private medical care alongside their award-winning internal mental health resources. In-house, online, and face-to-face mental health training is available to employees. In addition, Unilever subsidizes gym memberships and a physical activity program. The premise is that an employee is no more than one click, one call, or one chat away from help.

Yellow Goldfish – 24/7 support: Nikki Kirbell, UK Health and Wellbeing Manager at Unilever, shares, "Our mental health services include a personal resilience tool as a confidential online questionnaire, where people considered in need of support will then be triaged to speak to a professional and then potentially referred to counseling services. We also run Mental Health First Aid training for our line managers to reinforce our online training tools for our employees and managers on mental health awareness. All employees have free access to the Headspace mindfulness app and 24/7 access to the EAP for wellbeing support."

#4. HUFFINGTON POST AND SLEEPING ON THE JOB

Sleep is essential to your health. Not only because there are individual and company benefits but because it reduces the chance of adverse events from happening in the workplace. Well-rested individuals have better quality work because they have a better mood, are more focused, have better mental performance, and feel less fatigued at work. Sleep also reduces memory decline, workplace injury, cyberloafing, and unethical behavior, while lack of sleep increases the likelihood of obesity, heart disease, diabetes, and depression. Organizational leaders are beginning to mention the importance of sleep in their ability to thrive. Arianna Huffington has cited the importance of a regular sleep schedule in her life. She believes it allows her to lead and work at her highest capacity.

Yellow Goldfish – Nap rooms: The Huffington Post has created nap rooms and encourages their use. Even a few minutes of napping can significantly reduce the likelihood of an employee making a mistake at work. A number of the best leaders and innovators throughout history, including Leonardo da Vinci, Thomas Edison, Eleanor Roosevelt, and John F. Kennedy, relied on frequent naps.

#5. CVS AND CIGARETTES

Brothers Stanley and Sidney Goldstein and partner Ralph Hoagland opened the first CVS store in 1963 in Lowell, Massachusetts. CVS stands for Consumer Value Stores. The store sold health and beauty products. By 1964, the chain had grown to 17 stores, and in its third year, the company began operating stores with a pharmacy department. The company expanded rapidly both through growth and acquisition. In less than 50 years, over 75% of the US population lived within three miles of a store. In 2014, CVS renamed itself CVS Health and became a pharmacy innovation company that is reinventing pharmacy and healthcare.[46]

Yellow Goldfish - Kickin' Butts: In 2014, CVS Caremark made a bold move and stopped selling cigarettes and other tobacco products as part of becoming more of a health care provider than a primarily retail business. Stores now offer mini-clinics and health advice to aid customers in visiting its pharmacies. "We have about 26,000 pharmacists and nurse practitioners helping patients manage chronic

---

46 www.cvshealth.com/about/company-history

problems like high cholesterol, high blood pressure, and heart disease, all of which are linked to smoking," said Larry J. Merlo, chief executive of CVS. "We came to the decision that cigarettes and providing health care just don't go together in the same setting." CVS also created a web resource at http://www.cvs.com/quit-smoking. The company received over one million visits to the site in its first year. CVS Health's "Kickin Butts" move took away an estimated $2 billion in tobacco and related product sales,[47] but the move strongly fulfilled their purpose "to help people on their path to better health."

#6. REEBOK THINKING INSIDE THE BOX

Some organizations have a company gym. Others may subsidize or pay for gym fees. Reebok took this to the next level in 2010 by converting a brick warehouse at Reebok's headquarters into an employee exclusive CrossFit "box" or workout center with six coaches and extensive equipment. The box is called CrossFit One. Hundreds of employees take classes called WODs (Workout of the Day). This employee benefit reinforces the company's mission to get consumers moving. Participants lost over 4,000 pounds collectively during their first year.

ADDITIONAL WAYS TO INCREASE HEALTH

- **Serve Nappachinos** - Allow employees to take short (30-minute) naps during dips in circadian rhythm. These usually occur around 3-4 p.m. Naps longer than this can make employees groggy rather than refreshed and energized. Dan Pink recommends a slight addition to the power nap called the "Nappachino." According to several studies, drinking coffee before you take a nap will yield superior benefits to napping or drinking coffee alone, as they both

47 www.nytimes.com/2014/02/06/business/cvs-plans-to-end-sales-of-tobacco-products-by-october.html

reduce the buildup of Adenosine[48], which is what makes you feel sleepy. So next time you decide to take a nap, simply drink a cup of coffee beforehand, and you will wake up feeling refreshed and ready to take on the rest of the day.[49]

- **Provide Prayer and Meditation Rooms** - The online marketplace eBay offers both prayer and meditation rooms. Employees can sit in silence—in minimalist rooms decorated in earth tones, accented with comfy pillows, floor mats, and fragrant flower buds—to catch a few critical moments of solitude and to decompress from the myriad stresses of a workday.
- **Offer Breakfast and Bonding Time** – At Clif Bar, every week, the company assembles for a company breakfast. Bagels, fresh fruit, eggs, oatmeal, juice, bacon, and sausage are served. The team shares news, announcements, and a consumer's letter of the week.
- **Promote Mindfulness -** Promega offers a program called ESI (Emotional and Social intelligence) Bootcamp that helps employees learn skills for self-awareness in the form of empathy, discernment, and courage.
- **Do Walking Meetings** – AnswerLab's CEO schedules walk and talks with employees. They go outside for a walking meeting. These one-on-ones provide team members with an opportunity to share any concerns or ideas. In the Netherlands, VANAD has created several recommended nature-paths with different lengths based on the duration of the meeting.
- **Offer Healthy Food and Less Sugar**: Major companies are replacing vending machines, introducing healthy snacks, and helping their staff off sugar in a push to boost productivity.

48 https://en.wikipedia.org/wiki/Adenosine
49 www.blog.gethapi.me/lifehack-tip-07-recharge-your-energy-with-a-nappachino-8207b81106744

KPMG has introduced short modules on a healthy lifestyle and an eight-week corporate wellness program that addresses behavioral factors that contribute to excess added sugar intake and increased risk of chronic disease.

- **Produce and Sell Healthy Additive-Free Food** – Companies such as Whole Food Markets, Healthy People, Organix, and Go-Tan offer food free of artificial flavors, colorants, preservatives, or sweeteners, and MSG (monosodium glutamate).
- **Offer body products free of** parabens, preservatives, Sodium-Laurel-Sulfate-Free (SLS), Phthalate, and GMO, like Weleda does.
- **Reduce Secondhand Smoke and discourage smoke** – Offer smoke-free resorts and amusement parks or establishes smoke-free shifts/days so that non-smokers have the option to choose health. Ensure ashtrays and smoking areas are far enough from your doors and open windows so that your customers and employees can avoid secondhand smoke.

The "H" in H.A.P.P.I.N.E.S.S. stands for Health. Let's move on to the A.

CHAPTER 7

AUTONOMY

"Find the autonomy in your work. Autonomy is key to feeling good about the work you do, no matter what kind of work it is."

- Jean Chatzky

THIS CHAPTER IN FIVE SENSES

Vistas

Tulips

Song: *My Way* (Frank Sinatra)

Mint

Wind

TEDx Talk:
The Puzzle of Motivation | Dan Pink

THE "A" IN H.A.P.P.I.N.E.S.S. STANDS FOR AUTONOMY.

Autonomy is about feeling a sense of control over both work and life. Freedom and control over one's actions promote happiness. In the words of David Howitt of the Meriwether Group:

> Consider the thought, "I need more work-life balance." Is work not life? It's not like you leave your life to go to work. Inherent in the term is the notion they are two separate things. In your life, you do certain things, one of them being work. There is no such thing as work-life balance; there is just balance. We need to integrate both seamlessly. When we don't integrate, we miss opportunities by not connecting authentically with our consumers. We fail to see ways we can enhance our brand and products if we are being too linear. In this day and age, when we ignore what our communities are yearning for—soul, purpose, and passion—we become overworked, stressed out, tired, and suffer.

From the earliest day of SAS Institute, founder Dr. James Goodnight worked toward creating a fun place to work. He wanted an environment where the work itself was the biggest reward. A place that would harness creativity and provide all of the resources the employees would need. His mantra was the golden rule and merely treating people the way he would like to be treated. The entire approach can be summed up by an employees' quote in *Fast Company*[50], "You're given the freedom, the flexibility, and the resources to do your job. Because you're treated well, you treat the company well."

---

50 www.fastcompany,com

PSYCHOLOGY

We include under the "AUTONOMY" category the following universal human needs:

- Choice
- Enablement
- Empowerment
- Freedom
- Independence
- Space/ Solitude
- Time

Let's look at four *Yellow Goldfish* we found for this Yellow Factor.

#1. SEMCO AND TAKING CONTROL OF YOUR CAREER

Brazil's Semco is an excellent example of a democratic, open environment with minimal hierarchy. CEO Ricardo Semler heads the group of companies. According to British management guru Charles Handy, "The way he works—letting his employees choose what they do, where and when they do it, and even how they get paid—is too upside-down for most managers." Semler has created a culture that promotes autonomy for employees.

Yellow Goldfish – autonomy practices: Each business unit operates under its complete control. Here's a list of seven practices that promote autonomy at Semco:

1. There are no set work hours.
2. Workers set their own salary twice a year.

3. The financial books are completely transparent and available for all to see.

4. Employees are encouraged to move around the office. In fact, they are technically not allowed to sit at the same desk two days in a row, which eliminates the need for time tracking by management.

5. Employees can reduce their hours or job share given their state of life. They can also "retire a little at a time," taking time off during their working years and receiving proportional compensation in retirement. The program allows employees to spend time on activities that are important to them, like learning to play the violin or climbing a mountain.

6. Attendance at all company meetings became voluntary. If a meeting would become boring, people could leave without repercussions.

7. Semco believes that it is essential to meet people interested in working with it, even if this interest is not immediate or there are no current opportunities. This belief led them to create the program *Date Semco.* Suitable for prospective employees and current ones, each gets a chance to meet to determine if the fit is right.

#2. PATAGONIA AND THE BOARDROOM

Patagonia Inc., based in California, attracts outdoorsy types with its athletic clothing brand and laser-like focus on work-life balance. Autonomy and time away from the office aren't just tolerated here; they are required, according to Rob BonDurant, Patagonia's Vice President of Marketing and de facto culture guide. Patagonia employees enjoy what the company calls "Let My People Go Surfing" time, a period during any working day where employees can head outdoors to get their creative juices flowing. Of course, they can't abandon their duties or ditch a meeting, but popping out for an impromptu climb or bike ride is encouraged. Patagonia's flextime policies that originated from founder Yvon Chouinard, an outdoor enthusiast who founded the company in 1974, are good for employee morale and invaluable to the company.

In the words of BonDurant, "The time we spend outside the office helps us manage the storytelling process around our products. We're designing ski and surfing apparel, and we need to be traveling and trying things out." Employees can catch a good swell, go bouldering for an afternoon, pursue an education, or get home in time to greet the kids when they come down from the school bus. It's one thing to talk the talk, but Patagonia backs it up. According to *Whole Living*[51], the company encourages outdoor activities so much that it even has a place where employees can store their surfboards called "The Boardroom."

This flexibility allows the company to keep valuable employees who love their freedom and sports. The benefits package is generous but makes good business sense too. It offers comprehensive health insurance (to attract serious athletes to work in retail stores), and it provides on-site childcare (since parents are more productive if they're not worrying about the health and well-being of their

---

51 www.wholeliving.com/133935/best-company-perks

children). In the words of Yvon Chouinard in the book *Let My People Go Surfing*, "Work had to be enjoyable on a daily basis. We all had to come to work on the balls of our feet, going up the stairs two steps at a time. We needed to be surrounded by friends who could dress whatever way they wanted, even barefoot. We needed to have flex time to surf the waves when they were good, or ski the powder after a big snowstorm, or stay home and take care of a sick child. We needed to blur that distinction between work and play and family."

Yellow Goldfish – Sabbatical: Patagonia also allows employees to take off up to two months at full pay and work for environmental groups. Lisa Myers, who works on the company's giving programs, tracked wolves in Yellowstone National Park during her sabbatical. The company also pays 50% of her college expenses as she pursues a wildlife biology degree. "It's easy to go to work when you get paid to do what you love to do," says Myers.

#3. IDEO AND COLLABORATING FOR SOCIAL GOOD

After earning a master's degree from Stanford, David Kelley formed his design firm in 1978 with fellow student Dean Hovey. The group's first studio was a fly-infested office above a dress shop in nearby Palo Alto. They made their furnishings and covered the floors with a green patio carpet. Kelley had met Apple Computer Inc. founder Steve Jobs at Stanford, and by 1983, the group had designed the first commercially available computer mouse for Apple's Lisa computer. It was later used on the first Macintosh. A butter dish and the ball from a bottle of roll-on deodorant were among the building blocks for the first prototypes.

In mid-1991, David Kelley Design merged with ID Two and Matrix Product Design to form IDEO Product Development, Inc. ID Two's Bill Moggridge was the one who picked the name out of the dictionary, according to the book *The Art of Innovation*. "IDEO" is the combining form of the word "idea," as in "ideology" or "ideogram". Today the company has over 200 employees in multiple offices around the world.[52]

Yellow Goldfish – OpenIDEO: OpenIDEO is an open innovation platform by IDEO, where people from all corners of the world collaboratively tackle some of the most challenging global issues through launching challenges, programs, and other tailored experiences. A challenge is a three-to-five months collaborative process that focuses attention on the topic and creates a space for community members to contribute and build off each other. This approach is modeled on IDEO's design thinking methodology.[53]

#4. LADIES AND GENTLEMEN OF THE RITZ-CARLTON

Employees of the Ritz-Carlton are referred to as Ladies and Gentlemen. The motto of the hotel is Ladies and Gentlemen serving Ladies and Gentlemen. Ritz-Carlton employees are given great latitude and autonomy to delight guests by attending to their expressed and unexpressed wishes and needs.

Yellow Goldfish - $2,000 Rule: Beyond mere words, this ultra-attendance to needs is demonstrated through a promise from leadership to their teams. Any Lady or Gentleman [employee] may expense up to $2,000 per guest per day to ensure the full engagement of the guest. They can do so without first needing permission from hotel leadership. In theory, this generosity is inspired by the lifetime value of the customer for the brand. The average Ritz-Carlton guest will spend over $250,000 over their lifetime with the brand. By ensuring the continued loyalty of the guests, Ritz-Carlton stands to gain a lifetime of continued visits and recommendations to peers.

52 www.fundinguniverse.com/company-histories/ideo-inc-history/
53 www.ideo.com/post/a-platform-to-harness-collaboration-for-social-good

This commitment to service results in far more emotion than a mere business transaction.[54]

ADDITIONAL WAYS TO INCREASE AUTONOMY IN BUSINESS

- **Job crafting** - Job crafting can be a powerful tool for reenergizing and reimagining your role. The exercise involves redefining your job to incorporate your motives, strengths, and passions. The practice prompts you to visualize the job, map its elements, and reorganize them to suit you better. In this way, you can put personal touches on how you see and do your job. The benefits, according to Amy Wrzesniewski, Justin Berg, and Jane Dutton in Harvard Business Review,[55] is that you "gain a greater sense of control at work—which is especially critical at a time when you're probably working longer and harder and expecting to retire later. Perhaps job crafting's best feature is that it's driven by you, not by your supervisor."
- **Flexible Family Time** - Former Google Executive Marissa Mayer believes women are especially susceptible to burning out because they are faced with more demands in the home. She shared with Hanna Rosin in an interview for her book, *The End of Men: And the Rise of Women*[56], "What causes burnout is not working too hard. People can work arbitrarily hard for an arbitrary amount of time, but they will become resentful if work makes them miss things that are really important to them." Mayer provided an anecdote for how she kept one Google executive, whom she calls "Katy," from quitting.

54 Source: Alec Dalton, Global Quality Improvement Manager at Marriott
55 www.hbr.org/2010/06/managing-yourself-turn-the-job-you-have-into-the-job-you-want
56 www.amazon.com/gp/product/1594488045

Katy loved her job, and she loved her team, and she didn't mind staying late to help out. What was bothering Katy was something entirely different. Often, Katy confessed, she showed up late at her children's events because a meeting went overly long, for no substantial reason other than meetings tend to go long. And she hated having her children watch her walk in late. For Mayer, this was a no-brainer. She instituted a Katy-tailored rule. If Katy had told her earlier that she had to leave at four to get to a soccer game, then Mayer would make sure Katy could leave at four. Even if there were only five minutes left to a meeting, even if Google co-founder Sergey Brin himself was mid-sentence and expecting an answer from Katy, Mayer would say "Katy's gotta go," and Katy would walk out the door and answer the questions later by e mail after the kids were in bed. The key to sustaining loyalty in employees is making sure they get to do the things that are most important to them outside of work.[57]

- **Working towards happiness** – In the words of Dan Gilbert in the TED talk, "The Science of Happiness"[58]:

  We should have preferences that lead us into one future over another. But when those preferences drive us too hard and too fast because we have overrated the difference between these futures, we are at risk. When our ambition is bounded, it leads us to work joyfully. When our ambition is unbounded, it leads us to lie, to cheat, to steal, to hurt others, to sacrifice things of real value. When our fears are bounded, we're prudent, we're cautious, and we're thoughtful. When our fears are unbounded and overblown, we're reckless, and we're cowardly. The lesson I want to

57 www.businessinsider.com/marissa-mayer-tip-on-preventing-employee-burn-out-2012-9
58 www.ted.com/talks/dan_gilbert_asks_why_are_we_happy

> leave you with, from these data, is that our longings and our worries are both to some degree overblown, because we have within us the capacity to manufacture the very commodity we are constantly chasing [Happiness] when we choose experience.

The "A" in H.A.P.P.I.N.E.S.S. stands for Autonomy. Let's move on to the first P.

CHAPTER 8

PURPOSE

"Corporate purpose is at the confluence of strategy and values. It expresses the company's fundamentals - the raison d'être or overriding reason for existing. It is the end to which the strategy is directed."

– Richard Ellsworth

THIS CHAPTER IN FIVE SENSES

- Hot Air Balloon
- Peony
- Song: *Purpose* (Justin Bieber)
- Sweet
- Warm breeze

TEDx Talk:
Start with Why | Simon Sinek

THE FIRST "P" IN H.A.P.P.I.N.E.S.S. STANDS FOR PURPOSE.

Purpose is becoming the new black. We believe it's more than a trend or passing fad. Purpose is emerging as a guiding light that can help businesses navigate and thrive in the 21st century. According to the EY Beacon Institute *Pursuit of Purpose Study*, "Purpose—an aspirational reason for being that is grounded in humanity—is at the core of how many companies are responding to the business and societal challenges of today."

What can happen if you put purpose at the core of your business to help drive happiness? Here are ten benefits from the EY Study:

1. Purpose instills strategic clarity.
2. Purpose guides both short-term decisions and long-term strategy at every level of an organization, encouraging leaders to think about systems holistically.
3. Purpose guides choices about what not to do as well as what to do.
4. Purpose channels innovation.
5. Purpose is a force for and a response to transformation.
6. Purpose motivates people through meaning, not fear. It clarifies the long-term outcome, so people understand the need for change rather than feeling it is imposed upon them.
7. Purpose is also a response to societal pressures on business to transform, to address global challenges, and to take a longer-term, more comprehensive approach to growth and value.

8. Purpose taps a universal need to contribute, to feel part of society.
9. Purpose recognizes differences and diversity. Purpose builds bridges.
10. Purpose helps individuals/teams to work across silos to pursue a single, compelling aim.

PSYCHOLOGY

We include under the "PURPOSE" category the following universal human needs:

- Capacity
- Challenge
- Clarity
- Competence
- Consciousness
- Contribution
- Effectiveness
- Efficacy
- Enrich life
- Expression/ self-expression
- Faith/ Hope
- Growth/ Evolution
- Liberation/ Transformation

- Meaning
- Spirituality
- Stimulation
- To Matter

PURPOSE IN BUSINESS

Here are some statistics that make a case for embracing purpose in business:

- 90 percent of executives surveyed said their company understands the importance of purpose, but only 46 percent said it informs their strategic and operational decision-making. Source: EY[59]
- 86 percent of employees would consider leaving an employer whose values no longer met their expectations. Source: PriceWaterhouseCoopers[60]
- 58 percent of companies with a clearly articulated and understood purpose experienced growth of +10%. Source: 2016 Global Purpose Index[61]
- Purposeful, value-driven companies outperform their counterparts by a factor of 12.[62]

According to Gallup,[63] when it comes to communicating an organization's purpose to your employees, customers, and stakeholders, words don't matter nearly as much as actions do.

59 www.ey.com/Publication/vwLUAssets/ey-the-business-case-for-purpose/$FILE/ey-the-business-case-for-purpose.pdf
60 www.pwc.com/m1/en/services/consulting/documents/millennials-at-work.pdf
61 www.cdn.imperative.com/media/public/Global_Purpose_Index_2016.pdf
62 www.amazon.com/Corporate-Culture-Performance-John-Kotter/dp/1451655320
63 www.gallup.com/workplace/236573/company-purpose-lot-words.aspx

Companies need to find ways to bring purpose to life. Creating little things that can make a big difference for both employees and customers is one way to bring purpose to life. "It's easy to state a purpose and state a set of values. It's much harder to enact them in the organization because it requires you to continually search for consistency across many disciplines and many activities," says Michael Beer.

Let's look at four *Yellow Goldfish* we found for this Yellow Factor.

#1. BARRY-WEHMILLER AND INSPIRATIONAL LEADERSHIP

Barry-Wehmiller is an industry leader and the largest packaging and automation company in North America. The company has experienced twenty consecutive years of 20 percent compound growth in revenue and share value. With revenues over $1 billion, CEO Robert Chapman has focused on creating and sustaining an environment that brings out the best in people. Barry-Wehmiller[64] has a name for this strategy: Achieving Principled Results on Purpose. "When people thrive, companies thrive," says Chapman.[65]

Yellow Goldfish – Fostering a Better World: Chapman believes that the goal of management should be more significant than chasing profits. Your action shouldn't be about boosting the bottom-line but rather about fostering a better world. "I'd like to awaken this country to the fact that we're destroying the very thing that we should value: the opportunity to live together with meaning and purpose. Leaders have to step outside the daily issues surrounding profitability and say, 'What's this all about?' I talk to CEOs all the time, and everyone agrees with me, but they say it sounds too hard. I say, 'You bet it's

64 www.bizmanualz.com/empower-employees/inspirational-leadership-the-barry-wehmiller-story.html
65 www.inc.com/audacious-companies/scott-leibs/barry-wehmiller.html

hard to be a good steward of people, but what's the alternative? This is the fabric of life.'"

#2. BEN & JERRY'S AND CLIMATE JUSTICE

In 1978, good friends Ben Cohen and Jerry Greenfield decided to start a business together. The duo briefly considered bagels but found the equipment was too expensive. Instead, they opted for opening a shop featuring homemade ice cream in Burlington, Vermont. Armed with a five-dollar correspondence course about ice cream-making from Penn State, they renovated an old gas station into a store. On their first anniversary, the pair gave away free cones to thank customers of their new business, a practice that continues today at Ben & Jerry's Homemade Ice Cream stores. Their goal was to operate the company in a way that actively recognizes the central role that business plays in society by initiating innovative ways to improve the quality of life locally, nationally, and internationally.

Ben and Jerry were pioneers in developing a socially conscious business. They were proponents of the idea that a business needs to protect the environment. They're advocates for what they call Climate Justice. In their words:

> We live in a world where the effects of climate change are increasingly real; from melting ice caps to rampant forest fires, it can no longer be denied that human-made carbon pollution is affecting our fragile planet. The scientific evidence is settled; global warming is real and already impacting people around the world. The question now is, "What are we doing about it?" Every passing year, we see changing patterns of precipitation, including more intense rainfall events around the world, dramatic changes in the arctic, changes in agricultural growing seasons, and rising sea levels and ocean acidification. Some of these changes

> in our climate will have dramatic ecological and social consequences. The cruel irony of climate change is that people in the developing world, who can least afford to adapt to climate change, will pay the steepest price for the 200 years of industrialization and pollution from the developed world. It truly is an issue of climate justice.[66]

The company believes that we must take steps to reduce global greenhouse gas emissions dramatically – and to do it in a way that equitably shares the burdens and risks of climate change among the nations of the world. There is no quick fix to solve climate change, but the company advocates for:

- Divesting from fossil fuels.
- Increasing renewable energy sources.
- Putting a price on carbon pollution.
- Working with developing countries to invest in renewable energy

Yellow Goldfish - The Chunkinator: The company has calculated its carbon footprint and is working to reduce it. They are working with suppliers to reduce methane emissions from farms. They are changing to cleaner, greener freezers in the U.S., and at their factory in the Netherlands, they built the Chunkinator that helps power the factory by using ice cream bi-products. It's one step toward doing more. Ben & Jerry's aims to get to 100 percent clean energy at all of their U.S. sites by 2020.

---

66 http://www.benjerry.com/values/issues-we-care-about/climate-justice

#3. GREYSTON BAKERY AND NEW CHANCES

Bernie Glassman founded Greyston Bakery in 1982. Glassman recognized that employment is the gateway out of poverty and toward self-sufficiency. In 1982, he opened Greyston Bakery, giving the hard-to-employ a new chance at life. His open-hiring policy offered employment opportunities regardless of education, work history, or past social barriers, such as incarceration, homelessness, or drug use. Glassman became a trailblazer and started an Open Hiring movement. He believes there are benefits available to any responsible business with a commitment to its people and community. Over more than three decades of pioneering work, Greyston has overcome the risks associated with Open Hiring, risks that go along with any disruptive and innovative business practice. Other businesses can now enjoy the benefits of what Greyston has learned with vastly reduced risk.

Yellow Goldfish - Center for Open Hiring: The Center for Open Hiring is a collaborative learning space that evaluates, improves, and defines best practices. The Center facilitates the widespread adoption of Open Hiring and supports innovation in the delivery of community programs for employees and neighbors. The Center focuses on four program areas:

1. Social Innovation Lab

2. Greyston Institute

3. Open Hiring™ Association

4. Jobs and Skills Accelerator

#4. GOOGLE AND A WELCOMING WORKPLACE

Google didn't become a happy company by mistake. It's a product of thoughtful design, a strong purpose, and ultimately culture. Founders Larry Page and Sergey Brin set the groundwork for building Google. Larry Page elaborates in a *New York Times* article:

> We have somewhat of a social mission, and most other companies do not. I think that's why people like working for us and using our services... Companies' goals should be to make their employees so wealthy that they do not need to work, but choose to because they believe in the company... Hopefully, I believe in a world of abundance. In that world, many of our employees don't have to work, they're pretty wealthy, and they could probably go years without working. Why are they working? They're working because they like doing something and believe in what they're doing.

Yellow Goldfish – Alley Oop Hammer: Perhaps there is a deeper reason for Google creating a more welcoming and fulfilling workplace. Here is a quote from Founder Larry Page's Commencement Address at the University of Michigan in May 2009:

> My father's father worked in the Chevy plant in Flint, Michigan. He was an assembly line worker... My Grandpa used to carry an "Alley Oop" hammer—a heavy iron pipe with a hunk of lead melted on the end. The workers made them during the sit-down strikes to protect themselves. When I was growing up, we used that hammer whenever we needed to pound a stake or something into the ground. It is wonderful that most people don't need to carry a heavy blunt object for protection anymore. But just in case, I have it here.

It bears repeating. Larry Page's grandfather used to take a hammer to work for protection. A lead pipe with a hunk of metal melted at the end of it. We can only imagine this was a constant reminder of the quest for a happy workplace at Google.

ADDITIONAL WAYS TO INCREASE PURPOSE

- **Create a rallying cry or manifesto** - Danone created a manifesto for their employees. According to the company:

  > "By living our Manifesto, we carry forward our mission to bring health through food to as many people as possible and our dual project for business success and social progress, while reflecting our values of Humanism, Openness, Proximity, and Enthusiasm." It embodies our commitment to lead an Alimentation Revolution by supporting people to adopt healthier choices and lifestyles, and by caring about the health and wellness of Danone and Danoners, of our communities and our planet, of current and future generations.

- **Create Meaning** - How you approach your work might directly affect your level of job satisfaction and determine the meaning you find in employment. Some interesting research in work orientation comes from Dr. Amy Wrzesniewski, an Associate Professor of Organizational Behavior at Yale University's School of Management. Dr. Wrzesniewski and other researchers have been studying a classification system that can help you recognize your orientation toward your work and find ways to attain greater job satisfaction. There are three types: Job, Career, and Calling. Employees that see their position as a calling tend to find more meaning and satisfaction in their work.

The first "P" in H.A.P.P.I.N.E.S.S. stands for Purpose. Let's move on to the second P.

CHAPTER 9

PLAY

"The best way to cheer yourself up is

to try to cheer somebody else up."

- Mark Twain

THIS CHAPTER IN FIVE SENSES

- Balloon
- Bird of Paradise
- Song: *New Shoes* (Paolo Nutini)
- Bacon with Cotton Candy at *City Club Raleigh*
- Lego

TEDx Talk:
Play is more than fun | Stuart Brown

THE SECOND "P" IN H.A.P.P.I.N.E.S.S. STANDS FOR PLAY.

Why is it that when we play, we immediately feel joyful, we have fun in what we are doing, and we feel re-energized afterward?

One of the reasons is that we go back to our kid-like feelings when we had the freedom of exploring and learning through play, feeling that there were no other consequences than losing the game and learning through our mistakes. It was just fun. The focus was on the experience rather than on the result.

PSYCHOLOGY

We include under the "PLAY & CREATIVITY" category the following universal human needs:

- Adventure
- Discovery
- Flow
- Fun
- Humor / Laugh
- Inspiration
- Lightness
- Passion
- Spontaneity
- Variety/ Diversity

- Vitality/ Liveliness

SCIENCE AND RESEARCH

What is play?

Dr. Stuart Brown, author of *Play: How It Shapes the Brain, Opens the Imagination, and Invigorates the Soul*, defines play as "something done for its own sake. It's voluntary; it's pleasurable; it offers a sense of engagement; it takes you out of time. And the act itself is more important than the outcome."

Under Play, we cluster examples that include **Fun, Humor, Gamification,** and **Creativity**.

These elements are important because:

- **Play shapes our brain**, helps us deal with difficulties, helps us foster empathy, helps us navigate complex social groups, promotes mastery of our crafts, and it is at the core of creativity and innovation.[67]
- **Fun and play** have shaped history far more than one might assume because the human brain is predisposed to engineer discovery through play. Our brains work differently when we're playing. We suspend our disbelief, and our minds start to make previously unimagined associations. It's in this freewheeling and playful mode that our minds are at their most creative.[68]
- **Creativity** as "designing or discovery something new" is the secret of transforming activities so that they are rewarding in and of themselves.[69]
- **Creativity** has been recognized through history and across cultures as something inherently valued and has been something

67 *Play: How It Shapes the Brain, Opens the Imagination, and Invigorates the Soul* by Dr. Stuart Brown
68 *Wonderland: How Play Made the Modern World* by Steven Johnson
69 *Creativity: Flow & The psychology of discovery and invention* by Mihály Csíkszentmihályi

people do and pursue for its own sake, because it gives them a sense of purpose and helps them solve problems.[70]

- **Maintaining a sense of humor makes us resilient**—it helps us lift our gloom, diminish fear, threat, and tension, reduces the negative impact of stressful situations and helps us connect to others.[71]
- **Having fun together** creates connection and bonding. It also makes the experience more memorable and sharable.

CHEMISTRY

From a chemical point of view, "PLAY" makes us happy because:

- Whenever we experience surprise, encounter novelty, or discover something new, our brain gives us a shot of dopamine.
- Creatively solving problems gives a feeling of reward, which stimulates dopamine production.
- Having fun and real laughter makes us produce endorphins.
- Gamification and gamified experiences trigger all of the DOSE chemicals in the brain that influence our happiness (DOSE: **D**opamine, **O**xytocin, **S**erotonin, **E**ndorphins).

70 *10 keys to Happier Living* by Vanessa King
71 *10 Keys to Happier Living* by Vanessa King

PLAY IN BUSINESS

In business, two significant opportunities for play are:

- gamification
- fostering creativity and fun in the workplace

In an interview with *TechnologyAdvice*, Nicole Lazzaro, a world-renowned game designer, explained that gamified user experiences created with neuroscience in mind keep consumers coming back for more. Whether you design those experiences to keep employees returning to your learning management system for more gamified training or to keep readers revisiting your site for more gamified content, this scientifically-backed approach works. For this reason:

- gamification was expected to grow to a $5.5 billion industry by the end of 2018 and - at the time of writing this update in August 2020 - is projected to grow from USD 9.1 billion in 2020 to USD 30.7 billion by 2025[72]
- and businesses can benefit from including gamified experiences into their technology and offering[73].

When we play, we are less concerned about making mistakes, and we are more open and creative and can come up with solutions that we may not have identified otherwise. And we do so while having fun. This dynamic is a double win for customers and employees: when employees come up with new creative and fun ways to deliver a particular product or experience, they feel happy and fulfilled during the creation process and with the result of their creation; while customers who receive the fun product, service, or experience feel happier too.

---

72 www.marketsandmarkets.com/Market-Reports/gamification-market-991.html
73 www.technologyadvice.com/blog/information-technology/activate-chemicals-gamify-happiness-nicole-lazzaro/

Let's look at five examples of *Yellow Goldfish* we found for this Yellow Factor.

1. SOUTHWEST MAKES IT ALWAYS FUN

One company we have identified that excels at Play, Fun, and Humor is **Southwest Airlines**. More than 38 years ago, Rollin King and Herb Kelleher got together and decided to start a different kind of airline. They began with a straightforward notion: If you get your passengers to their destinations when they want to get there, on time, at the lowest possible fares, and **make darn sure they have a good time doing it, people will fly your airline**. On June 18, 1971, the love airline was born.[74]

Now forty-seven years later, there are countless examples of how they made sure people have a good time flying with them, and their success proves their simple notion was correct. There are remarkable stories we discovered about them as we collected our examples. Check them out in Listly by searching keyword Southwest. Here are three examples of creating Southwest-style happiness by:

- using the intercom to congratulate a couple on a flight which was getting married the next day and then inviting others to extend well wishes or advice about what they've learned in their own relationships by writing it down on cocktail napkins, which were then collected and handed to the couple as the plane's wedding gift to them;[75]
- using the power of music to make a positive difference and to be the bright spot in someone's day by playing the ukulele;[76]
- surprising newlyweds on their flight to their honeymoon destination with a mid-flight 'wedding' ceremony and instructing

---

74 www.southwest.com/html/about-southwest/

75 Jeanne Bliss podcast THE CHIEF CUSTOMER OFFICER HUMAN DUCT TAPE SHOW episode 91 www.customerbliss.com/create-power-moments-dan-heath/

76 www.southwest.fm/southwest-music-scene/a-man-and-a-ukulele/

them to repeat a set of Southwest-inspired vows: "We vow to love each other, only fly Southwest, and to always put our small carry-on bags underneath the seat and not in the overhead bins," said the flight attendant with the couple echoing every word.[77]

Yellow Goldfish - funny flight safety announcements: "Put the oxygen mask on yourself first, and then place it on your child. If you are traveling with more than one child, start with the one with the greatest earning potential." "If you should get to use the life vest in a real-life situation, the vest is yours to keep." "Please pass all the plastic cups to the center aisle so we can wash them out and use them for the next group of passengers."

These memorable flight announcements from Southwest Airlines are just one example of how Southwest has become a leader in customer loyalty. Some statements have gone viral over the years and are even displayed on a "wall of fame" at Southwest's Headquarters to commemorate the best jokes.

So, what are Southwest's funny flight safety announcements worth?

By injecting fun, creativity, and recognition into everyday experiences, humorous announcements measurably increase happiness and loyalty. Because the laughter usually generated by these hilarious announcements stimulates the production of endorphins, these announcements have a real impact on customer happiness. They actually reduce the stress traveling brings—even if a person is not afraid of flying—and enable passengers to be more relaxed during the flight, potentially changing their entire perception of the experience. This approach sounds good, but what does hard data say about the value of these announcements?

---

77 www.foxnews.com/travel/2017/08/09/southwest-surprises-newlyweds-with-mid-flight-wedding-ceremony.html

In *The Power of Moments: Why Certain Experiences Have Extraordinary Impact,* Dan and Chip Heath explain how and why Southwest's flight attendants try to have fun even in the boring part of the job, like making the safety announcements, and they looked at data from the Southwest's analytics team to determine the impact of the announcements. The effect was quite clear.

In the company's customer satisfaction surveys, about 1 in every 70 customer respondents mentioned the flight safety announcement as one of the most memorable aspects of their flights. Looking only at loyal customers (the ones who fly more than once per year), they discovered that customers on flights with a funny announcement flew on average one-half flight more than the ones who hadn't heard a funny statement. The insights team concluded that by doubling the number of customers who listen to the announcements, the company could earn an additional $140 million **a year** in incremental revenue because of loyalty stimulation.

That's quite an impressive return on investment, considering that it doesn't require any real financial investment at all. Just an astonishing ROM: Return on Moment!

2. COOLBLUE SPRINKLES EVERYTHING WITH HUMOR & CREATIVITY

Coolblue is a Dutch e-commerce company founded in 1999 by Pieter Zwart (CEO), Paul de Jong, and Bart Kuijpers. The company operates over 300 individual webshops and eight physical shops under the Coolblue brand. In 2016, Coolblue reported it sold 857 million euros worth of goods, a 55 percent increase compared to the previous year.[78]

---

78 www.en.wikipedia.org/wiki/Coolblue

The Coolblue tagline and brand promise is "Everything for a smile" (*Alles for a glimlach* in Dutch), and they surely fulfill that with 96 percent customer satisfaction only by "Doing something more than the customer expects from you."

Here are some of the fun things Coolblue does to exceed expectations:

- Make Terms and Conditions clear, but also outright funny
- Create clever, funny product descriptions that always include pros and cons
- Provide a "wait therapy"—when you submit your online order, they turn the waiting time till your order arrives into fun by giving you three options: 1) a door hanger to let others know you are waiting, 2) a link to a music playlist, or 3) the option to put your feet on the table, lean back, close your eyes, and relax.
- Ship the purchase in a fun, colorful box that even humorously describes the ingredients of the box and packing material ("your order, wood pulp, paper, colorants Pantone 2925C & 021C, bubble plastic, a bit of specialism and of course a lot of love"), the ten steps for mindful opening and a "thank you" for the neighbor in case he got the delivery on your behalf (see in the photo a collage of various parts of the box)
- Send customers a personal message on actual postcards
- Provide following day delivery, as long as you order by 23:59 (which Rosaria does very often, and Stan probably would too if they were also serving the US). Delivery is always free, even on Sunday.
- Invite you to share what type of "package opener" you are
- Invite you to "up-cycle" the box and send the photo of your artwork for the monthly "FOTO CHALLENGE"

- And on a customer's birthday? They don't just send an ordinary email with a coupon code. Instead, they send a pdf file of a birthday festoon that can be printed, cut, and hang following their funny instructions, which include "Party."

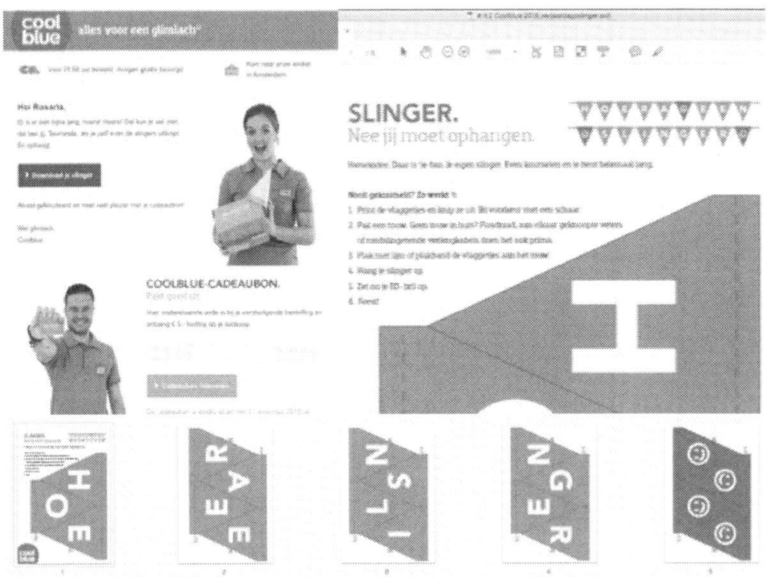

Photos & images credit: Rosaria Cirillo Louwman

3. WOOHOO AND "THE WOOHOO ACCOUNT" MONTHLY BUDGET FOR FUN

Alexander Kjerulf, CEO of Woohoo and author of *Happy Hour is 9 to 5,* shares how Woohoo "happily walks the talk about fun" in his latest book *Leading with Happiness: How the Best Leaders Put Happiness First to Create Phenomenal Business Results and a Better World.* From the book:

> Having fun is a great way to make customers happy and connect with them. Exactly how to do it depends on your team and what business you're in. The vast majority of workplaces offer at least some potential for having plain old fun with the customers, which, when done right, can brighten a lot of people's day. At Woohoo we have a monthly budget called The Woohoo Account for having fun with customers, partners, and suppliers. We've invited them to things like a movie at a local cinema (incidentally, we showed "Horrible Bosses," which is hilarious), a backstage tour of the national aquarium, and a huge party featuring the world's happiest DJ.

4. PEPPERCOMM AND COMEDY TRAINING

At Peppercomm, comedy training is mandatory and part of the onboarding process. The training consists of learning about different types of comedy, such as observational humor. It's also become a great way to meet the new hires with graduation from the training consisting of a five-minute set of stand-ups.

Deborah Brown, Partner and Managing Director, credits humor with improving productivity, building teamwork, and injecting fun into the agency. Humor is now part of the fabric of Peppercomm, whether it takes the form of spicing up an interoffice e-mail or creating a funny video for a client pitch. The agency has received several positive stories in the press and has recently started to extend the training to existing and prospective clients.

The agency was recognized by *Crain's* as one to the Top 50 places to work in New York City.[79] Their approach of taking the business but not yourself seriously can be summed up in one quote from the agency:

> Comedy training does more than creating a unique culture. It produces a better business executive, someone who is just a tad ahead of their peers when it comes to listening skills, building audience rapport, and thinking in a nanosecond. Happy, funny employees are also the reason why we maintain so many long-term client relationships, experience low turnover, and produce amazing creativity. And that's no joke.

5. DEEN SUPERMARKTEN AND FUN, ENGAGING LOYALTY CAMPAIGNS

DEEN Supermarkten in the Netherlands has already run several campaigns that engage kids, parents, and the local community in some fun:

- **Local football team sticker cards**: Many supermarkets regularly run sticker card loyalty collections (e.g., one envelope of sticker cards every 10€ of shopping), and often they involve soccer /football players.

---

79 www.purplegoldfish.com/employee-engagement-is-a-laughing-matter-peppercom/

DEEN chose local neighborhood club football players for their cards, so every envelope was a chance for the kids to discover if there were any stickers from their classmates and for the parents to learn "the story" about neighborhood kids.

- **Jurassic World collection**: In this variation of one envelope for every 10€ of shopping, the envelope contained four dinosaur sticker cards and either two tattoos or two sticker points to get a hand puppet in the shape of a dinosaur's mouth for 2.50€. Kids have fun collecting the dinosaur puppet, which makes the parents happy too. The employees enjoy seeing kids so cheerful, and neighborhood parents/family meet at the supermarket to get the stickers. People without kids happily handed over their envelopes to the kids, enjoying how something so simple could spark so much joy and excitement.

Photo credit: Rosaria Cirillo Louwman

ADDITIONAL WAYS TO INCREASE PLAY

- **Offer games.** In hospitality areas, add handheld games and board games for your customers. *Farmcamp*, a farm resort, has a chest full of board games for kids and families.
- **Fulfill customers' dreams engaging in unexpected playfulness.** In his article "*5 Wow Customer Service Stories from*

5-Star Hotels,"[80] Micah Solomon shares a brilliant example. When Micah answered the question, "Is there anything else I can help you with?" saying, "I've always wanted a pony." the concierge of Four Seasons Hotel in Austin, Texas, truly surprised him. Micah shares: "The concierge followed up within minutes with four printed pages, in color, of horses available for purchase within twenty-five miles, that she slipped under my door, with an offer to pick up any that I fancied, assuming my credit card could hold the damage."

- **Use gamification to engage your customers**. With the Nike+ system, Nike has attracted the largest community of runners ever assembled. At the same time, they learned things about their customers' habits that they had not known before:[81] more than 1.2 million runners have collectively tracked more than 130 million miles and burned more than 13 billion calories.
- **Make your product packaging engaging**. Bloomon (a flowers' delivery subscription company in the Netherlands) has made unpacking the weekly flowers an experience in itself with the wrap full of tips and jokes about the flowers—guaranteed to bring an extra cheery smile to your face.
- **Explore the creative power of intuitive painting during your next team event.** An Intuitive Painting work session not only is excellent for team building, but it can also unleash creativity and bring up very innovative solutions[82].

The second "P" in H.A.P.P.I.N.E.S.S. stands for Play... Let's move on to the I…

---

80 www-forbes-com.cdn.ampproject.org/c/s/www.forbes.com/sites/micahsolomon/2017/07/29/5-wow-customer-service-stories-from-5-star-hotels-examples-any-business-can-learn-from/amp/
81 www.wired.com/2009/06/lbnp-nike/
82 SmART, How Art Inspires Action in Business, by Daniella Rubonovitz

CHAPTER 10

INTEGRITY

"The greatness of a man is not in how much wealth he acquires, but in his integrity and his ability to affect those around him positively."
- Bob Marle

THIS CHAPTER IN FIVE SENSES

- Blue Sky
- Oak
- Song: *Respect* (Aretha Franklin)
- Water
- Rope

TEDx Talk:
Paving the Path to Integrity, Peace and Happiness
Dr. Bashir Jiwani, PhD

THE "I" IN H.A.P.P.I.N.E.S.S. STANDS FOR INTEGRITY.

Happy employees are foundational to happy customers. Study after study proves that happy teams are more creative, productive, and effective. Just think about it for a second. Happy employees are friendlier to be around; they like making their customers happy, and therefore they work harder to achieve that. Happy customers spend more money, are more loyal to a brand, and tell their friends and family. It's a marketing plan in itself. Further, when you found or lead your company, you should aim to foster this atmosphere, so that working with people you like on a business you believe in means everyone can work together toward a common, meaningful goal.[83]

PSYCHOLOGY

We include under the "INTEGRITY & HONESTY" category the following universal human needs:

- Authenticity
- Effectiveness
- Feedback
- Justice
- Presence
- Progress
- Quality

83 www.thehappystartupschool.com/blog/2015/9/29/why-happiness-should-be-your-business-model

- Reflection
- Sincerity
- Transparency

Let's look at five examples of *Yellow Goldfish* we found for Integrity.

#1. TONY'S CHOCOLONELY AND BEAN TO BAR SLAVE-FREE CHOCOLATE

Tony's Chocolonely has grown to be the largest Dutch chocolate company in less than ten years. It entered the U.S. market in 2016 and later also Belgium, Denmark, Sweden, and Germany. The company was started by Dutch journalist Teun van de Keuken when he discovered that cocoa was being bought from plantations that used child slavery. After learning these facts, Tuen "Tony" ate a dozen chocolate bars and turned himself into the police. When the trial didn't result in his conviction for buying an illegal product, he decided to start his own chocolate company exclusively focused on providing slave-free chocolate to the industry.

In today's free-trade world, slaves are still at work on cocoa farms in West Africa, many of them children. According to Tony's Chocolonely website,[84] the company exists to change this situation by making 100 percent slave-free the norm in the chocolate industry. They are out to show that chocolate can be made with integrity, through direct, long-term relationships with cocoa farmers and other supply chain partners.

Tony's Chocolonely has created a completely transparent and traceable bean-to-bar process, where they agree on better prices for

---

84 www.tonyschocolonely.com/us/en

the farmers. The brand also provides business and agricultural training to increase productivity on their farms.

Yellow Goldfish – Chocolonely Foundation: One percent of Tony Chocolonely's net revenue is donated to the Chocolonely Foundation. The Foundation supports projects to eradicate slavery in the cocoa supply chain. When you unwrap the brightly colored wrapper on Tony's Chocolonely, it evokes a sense of perhaps this is what a Willy Wonka chocolate bar would be like, looking for the golden ticket. Then you discover a six-ounce chunky bar that's unequally divided to illustrate the inequality in the chocolate industry. And at the time of our update in August 2020, Tony's is actually busy building, just outside Amsterdam, a Willy Wonka style factory where their HQ employees will be based, and their customers will be able to have a rollercoaster tour. A great example of "Play" *Yellow Goldfish.*

#2. SOUTHWEST AIRLINES AND CULTURE

Southwest Airlines arguably has the best quality and on-time performance figures for any airline. The airline's success is often attributed to Herb Kelleher's quirky leadership, which shaped Southwest's culture into one which values humor, altruism, and trust.

Yellow Goldfish – Mutual Respect: In her book *The Southwest Airlines Way*, Jody Gittell points to high-performance relationships based around shared goals, shared knowledge, mutual respect, and frequent and effective communication. She cites these elements of integrity as the real underlying reasons for their success. "If employees are treated right, they treat the outside world right, the outside world uses the company's product again, and that makes the shareholders happy," says Herb Kelleher.

Peggy Uhle was boarding a flight from Chicago's Midway Airport to Columbus, Ohio. She turned off her cell phone as the plane rolled away from the gate (talk about an observant passenger). Just before take-off, the plane turned around and taxied back to the gate. Southwest had received an emergency call from Peggy's husband with an urgent message about a severe injury to their 24-year-old son. Her husband had not been able to reach her directly since her phone was turned off. While Peggy was trying to process this information, Southwest reticketed her on the next direct flight to Denver, where her son was, and arranged all of the other details for her. All for free.

In an interview with BoardingArea.com, Peggy explained more, "They offered a private waiting area, rerouted my luggage, allowed me to board first, and packed a lunch for when I got off the plane in Denver. My luggage was delivered to where I was staying, and I even received a call from Southwest asking how my son was doing."

Luckily, her son has reportedly recovered from his injuries making for a happy ending to the story. While we can't prepare ourselves for the unexpected in life, it's nice to know companies like Southwest Airlines can help make a difficult situation a little less complicated when we need it the most.

#3. NEW BELGIUM BREWING AND CORE VALUES

Jeff Lebesch traveled to Europe in the summer of 1988 and toured Belgium on his mountain bike. He returned home to Colorado, changed by the experience. Three years later, in the basement of his house, the electrical engineer installed some brewing equipment. It was there that Jeff created his first two Belgian-style beers. The first was a brown double named Abbey and an amber named in honor of his mountain bike. In Colorado, mountain bikes are called Fat Tires. Jeff's wife, Kim Jordan, became New Belgium's first bottler, sales rep, distributor, marketer, and financial planner. By the summer of 1991, the duo was selling Abbey and Fat Tire at festivals on the weekends. Less than one year later, the pair quit their day jobs and moved production out of their basement. New Belgium Brewing

Company[85] was born. Before the first bottle of beer was ever sold, Jeff and Kim defined a clear purpose for New Belgium: *"To manifest our love and talent by crafting our customers' favorite brands and proving business can be a force for good."* The pair hiked into Rocky Mountain National Park with a jug of homebrew in one hand and pen/pad in the other. Here's what they wrote:

COMPANY CORE VALUES AND BELIEFS

- Remembering that we are incredibly lucky to create something fine that enhances people's lives while surpassing our consumers' expectations.
- Producing world-class beers.
- Promoting beer culture and the responsible enjoyment of beer.
- Kindling social, environmental, and cultural change as a business role model.
- Environmental stewardship: Honoring nature at every turn of the business.
- Cultivating potential through learning, high involvement culture, and the pursuit of opportunities.
- Balancing the myriad needs of the company, our coworkers and their families.
- Trusting each other and committing to authentic relationships and communications.
- Continuous, innovative quality, and efficiency improvements.
- Having fun.

---

85 www.newbelgium.com/Brewery/company/history

Yellow Goldfish - Beer Scouts: The Beer Scouts are an interdepartmental group who sponsor volunteer events for coworkers and community members as a means to give back and inspire positive change. The group was formed to connect busy people to projects they are passionate about. The Scouts work to find great causes that are aligned with New Belgium's values to support each year. They have helped log 12,500 volunteer hours of coworker time in the past five years. The New Belgium Scouts encourage all co-workers to find causes that they are passionate about to dedicate the precious gift of time to on their own, and then they reward employees with paid time off for their efforts. Employees receive one hour of PTO for every two hours of volunteer work. In 2015, New Belgium coworkers volunteered[86] over 2,773 hours.

#4. INNOCENT DRINKS AND THE BIG KNIT

London-based Innocent came up with an inventive idea that involves their customers directly in charity. The program called the Big Knit[87] involves knitting little hats to raise money to help keep older people warm in winter. As Alexander Kjerulf describes in his book, *Leading With Happiness*, people are invited to knit hats that will fit on the caps of Innocent's small smoothie bottles and send them to the company. Innocent collects all the hats and puts them on smoothie bottles that are then sold in stores, and donates 25 pence for every hat to a charity called Age UK, which helps the elderly. The Big Knit website even features a section called "Meet the Knitters," where they celebrate some of their top knitters, including two lovely retired teachers named Ali and Marion from Gosport. They have so far contributed a whopping 2,500 little hats between them.

86 www.newbelgium.com/Sustainability/Community/BeerScouts
87 www.thebigknit.co.uk/

#5. PLASTICITY AND THE HERO GENERATION

Plasticity[88] works with schools and educators to help youth develop their HERO GEM traits (Hope, Efficacy, Resilience, Optimism, Gratitude, Empathy, Mindfulness). The purpose of the project is to improve well-being for elementary school students and their teachers and demonstrate that higher social-emotional skills contribute to improved personal and academic wellbeing.

"To combat the negative impacts of stress on our lives we need to emphasize a future of mental health prevention and optimization through psychological fitness. HERO Generation will enhance the ongoing efforts to make schools psychologically safe and higher-performing environments for students, staff, caregivers, and communities."

ADDITIONAL WAYS TO INCREASE INTEGRITY

- **Become a force for good** – The B Corp community works toward reduced inequality, lower levels of poverty, a healthier environment, stronger communities, and the creation of more high-quality jobs with dignity and purpose. By harnessing the power of business, B Corps use profits and growth as a means to a greater end: positive impact for their employees, communities, and the environment.[89]
- **Sign the Giving Pledge[90] as an individual leader or pledge 1%[91] as an organization** - Pledge 1% encourages and challenges companies to commit 1 percent of equity, product, and employee time for their communities because pledging a small portion of future success can have a significant impact on tomorrow.

The "I" in H.A.P.P.I.N.E.S.S. stands for Integrity... Let's move on to the N…

---

88 www.plasticitylabs.com/hero-generation/
89 www. bcorporation.eu/about-b-corps
90 www. givingpledge.org/
91 www. pledge1percent.org/

CHAPTER 11

NATURE

"The best and most beautiful things in the world cannot be seen or even touched. They must be felt with the heart."

– Helen Keller

THIS CHAPTER IN FIVE SENSES

- Trees
- Jasmin
- Song: *I Got Sunshine* (Avery)
- Strawberry
- Sand

TEDx Talk:

Where Joy Hides and How to Find It

Ingrid Fetell Lee

THE "N" IN H.A.P.P.I.N.E.S.S. STANDS FOR NATURE.

When we are in nature, whether it's at sea, on a lake, in the forest, or on a mountain, we immediately feel a sense of happiness, fulfillment, joy, peace with ourselves and the universe. Why is this? The moment that we are in nature, we move from thinking to feeling. Nature allows us to perceive the reality around us through our five senses:

- **Sight**: the vastness of the sea, the rhythm of waves, the serene beauty of a lake, of the majesty of a forest, the landscapes of a mountain
- **Smell**: the tang of the sea, the hint of pine and spruce, the fragrance of wild berries, grass and flowers, the clean crispness of mountain air
- **Sound**: the waves against the shore, the rustle of leaves, the songs of birds, and the silence of the mountain
- **Taste**: salt on our lips at the beach, gathered nuts and berries, freshly picked garden bounty
- **Touch**: the feel of sand or grass under our feet, smooth river or lake rocks, water as we immerse ourselves or splash, the crunch of fall leaves underfoot, the coldness of snow, the slipperiness of ice, silky petals of spring and summer flowers

So, how can companies recreate the sensations of nature for customers and employees? How can companies recreate those feelings of beauty and harmony found in nature?

Let's look at what science, psychology, and chemistry have to say.

SCIENCE AND RESEARCH

In her TEDx Talk "*Where Joy Hides and How to Find It,*"[92] Ingrid Fetell Lee, designer and author of *Joyful*[93], describes her 10-year journey to understand how an intangible concept like *joy* could manifest in the tangible, physical world. Her key finding was that "the physical world can be a powerful resource to us in creating happier, healthier lives."

Lee explains that while happiness is a measure of how good we feel over time, joy is about what makes us feel good in the present moment. Joy can be found in the simple things you've most likely decided you were too old for. Still, joy also can be accessed through physical attributes like bright colors or fun patterns, and therefore, it can be fully integrated into our everyday life. Lee shares the results of schools painted by Publicolor. Their administrators report[94] that when their schools get a dose of bright color, they see attendance improve, graffiti disappear, and kids report feeling safer.

Research[95] has found that people who work in more colorful offices are more alert, more confident, and friendlier than those working in gray spaces. Why? Possibly because of a connection to our evolution. *Color*, in a very primal way, is a sign of life, a symbol of energy. And the same is true of:

- *Abundance*: we evolved in a world where scarcity is dangerous, and abundance means survival.
- *Rounded shapes* (as opposed to sharp-pointed forms): our brain associates sharpness to danger, likely because angles in nature are often associated with objects that might be dangerous to us, and

92 Video on YouTube www.youtu.be/A_u2WFTfbcg
93 Joyful: The Surprising Power of Ordinary Things to Create Extraordinary Happiness by Ingrid Fetell Lee
94 www.publicolor.org/results/statistics/
95 www.ncbi.nlm.nih.gov/pubmed/17050390

lights up the amygdala, a part of the brain associated with fear and anxiety.

Next to the design and beauty element of nature, there is also harmony and wellbeing to consider.

Many studies link our health and well-being to the natural world. In fact, a whole new field of *ecopsychology* has emerged, combining the efforts of ecologists, psychologists, spiritualists, philosophers, and others, to "explore the synergistic relationship between personal health and well-being and the health and well-being of our home, the Earth."[96]

In her book *The Nature Fix: Why Nature Makes Us Happier, Healthier and More Creative*, Florence Williams explains that natural spaces—even citified versions of them—can help us feel psychologically restored, and they make us healthier, more creative, more empathetic, and more apt to engage with the world and with each other. Nature, it turns out, is good for civilization. Researchers in Finland[97] measured people's well-being in three different environments: urban streetscapes, busy city parks, and wilder forests and found that just 15 to 45 minutes of sitting outside in both the park and forest or taking a short walk in these settings made people feel more psychologically restored, relaxed, vital, and creative than their urban-street side peers.

Nature is the best teacher for new design approaches, not only for delight but also for a sustainable economy. A biomimicry revolution is on the horizon. You can read more about this exciting concept on www.view.ingwb.com/the-need-for-natural-design.

---

96 www.psychologytoday.com/intl/blog/the-moment-youth/201403/does-nature-make-us-happy
97 Team led by Liisa Tyrvainen of the Finnish Forest Research Institute

PSYCHOLOGY

Not only nature activates and gets us in touch with our five senses, but it also meets our deepest human needs for:

- **Beauty,** with all of its colors, shapes, and duplications of the same elements, which gives us a feeling of abundance and are pleasant to the eye.
- **Harmony,** because everything seems to be making perfect sense precisely as it is. For example, the way that the waves shape the shore as they retire always appears beautiful and perfect.

We include under the "NATURE, BEAUTY & HARMONY" category the following universal human needs:

- Calm / Relaxation
- Comfort
- Communion
- Completion
- Ease
- Equality / Fairness
- Integration
- Peace
- Predictability
- Respect
- Stability/ Balance

Meeting any of these needs will release dopamine, the "reward molecule." Let's also look at what different chemicals nature, beauty, and harmony release.

CHEMISTRY

From a neurochemical point of view, spending time in nature supports our physical and mental well-being because:

- It stimulates the production of endorphin ("The Pain-killing Molecule") and helps us regulate emotions.
- It's associated with pursuing an activity, like reaching the top of the hill, which stimulates the production of serotonin ("The Confidence Molecule") and adrenaline ("The Energy Molecule").

Research has confirmed that just a fifty-minute walk in a natural setting results in decreased anxiety and negative emotions and preserves positive well-being as well as improves cognitive benefits like increased working memory performance.[98]

NATURE AND BEAUTY IN BUSINESS

We found that organizations can recreate the same perceptions, feelings, and benefits of immersing in nature through the following two ways:

1. **Delight by Design:**

a. recreate the nature experience by appealing to any or all of the five senses

b. add beauty and harmony in the design of both workspace and products

---

98 www.sciencedirect.com/science/article/pii/S0169204615000286

2. **Experience and Preserve Nature:** encourage, create, and even enable the opportunity for customers and employees to spend more time outdoors in nature, and to respect and preserve the environment

Let's look at six *Yellow Yellow Goldfish* we found for this Yellow Factor in both areas. Given the sensory nature of this category, when we say "look," this time, we genuinely mean "look"! For this part, you'll find fewer words and more images. We want to delight you by design too!

1. DELIGHT BY DESIGN

#1. GE AND ITS MRI SCAN TURNED INTO AN ADVENTURE EXPERIENCE FOR KIDS

Diagnostic imaging procedures are cutting-edge technology, but at the same time, they are an unpleasant experience for patients—and even more so for pediatric patients. Doug Dietz is an industrial designer who has worked for GE healthcare for 20 years. After an eye-opening moment in a hospital corridor, Dietz created a scanner experience that not only didn't frighten children but provided them with an adventure and enabled a different type of connection and "conversations on the way back home" for that family.

In his TEDx talk, he powerfully and vulnerably explains the power of Empathy as a much needed first step to design and goes on to say, "when you design for meaning, good things will happen." In the HOW chapter, we will explore this example in more detail.

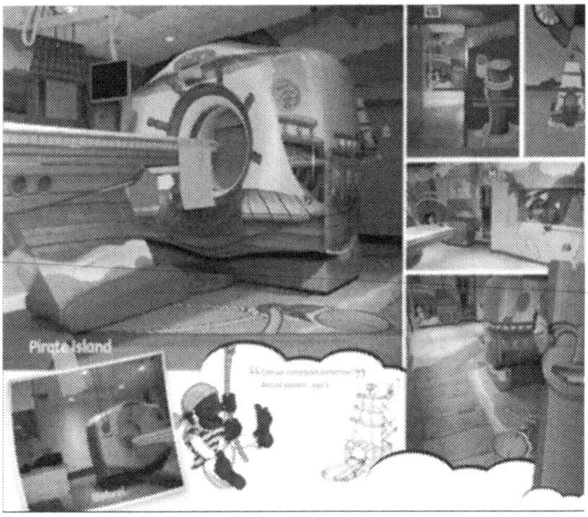

Photo credit: Transforming healthcare for children and their families: Doug Dietz at TEDxSanJoseCA 2012[99]

#2. ZAANS MEDISCH CENTRUM AND ITS SLIDE, PIANO, AND PLENTY OF ART

Photo credit: Rosaria Cirillo Louwman

Zaans Medical Centre is the first lean hospital in the Netherlands. It is an efficient and compact building where professional healthcare and a personal approach strengthen each other in the care given. Architecture, urbanism, landscape, and interior are brought together in a coherent design. Clear routing, an abundance of daylight, and positive distractions

99 www.youtube.com/watch?v=jajduxPD6H4

contribute to an environment that does not feel like a hospital but instead feels like a place that promotes well-being.[100]

#3. SANIFAIR AND ITS GERMAN HIGHWAY KIDS FRIENDLY RESTROOMS

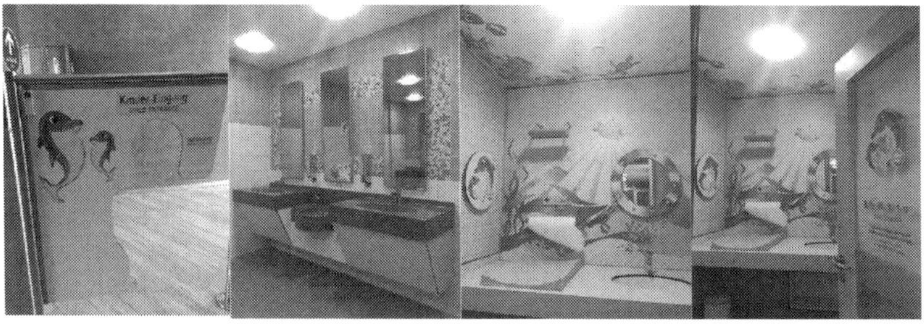

Photo credit: Rosaria Cirillo Louwman

SANIFAIR offers self-cleaning, barrier-free toilets at motorway service stations and filling stations. They make traveling with children more comfortable and add a bit of fun to pit-stop visits. There are unusual kid-height sinks, so parents don't have to lift or hold the child. The baby changing room is like a trip to discovery land, well stocked with supplies and decorated with colors and images to keep baby and older brothers/sisters fascinated during the diaper change. When traveling from the Netherlands to Italy, Rosaria's family chooses their travel route through Germany as much as possible because the highway station rest areas enable a more relaxed journey while their playgrounds add a bit of fun with colorful and playful architectural designs.

100 You can see more photos on www.mecanoo.nl/Projects/project/71/Zaans-Medical-Centre-and-Health-Boulevard

ADDITIONAL WAYS TO DELIGHT BY DESIGN

Check out our List.ly collection (using the search function) for examples to:

- **Make your toilets worth a visit -** At AFAS software (the Netherlands), the toilet doors' inside have a real size photo of a gentleman handing you a red roses bouquet; at Neunkirchen Zoo (Germany,) the toilets have beautiful artistic tiles' decoration; and many companies make male/female signs consistent with their brand and experience.
- **Make your office entrance memorable -** The Salesforce HQ in San Francisco has a 106-foot-long lobby screen containing nearly seven million pixels! With the switch of a button, the screen turns the lobby into a dramatic and beautiful waterfall scene. The digital signage completely transforms the space from an average interior to a cascading waterfall that breaks over the door frames.
- **Create offices where everyone enjoys spending time -** At Coolblue, each meeting room has a theme, and the employees are full of praise for this innovative work environment.
- **Create schools that feel joyful and secure -** After the mass shooting at Sandy Hook Elementary School in 2012, the architects Svigals + Partners knew that they needed to create a secure building, but they wanted to make one that was also joyful.[101] The use of impressive building materials, an unusual architectural design, and colorful concrete blocks and decorative touches work "to give everything a joyful or colorful touch," explains project manager Julia McFadden.[102]

---

101 See images on www.svigals.com/project/sandy-hook-school-newtown-ct/
102 www.architecturalrecord.com/articles/11839-a-new-chapter-for-the-sandy-hook-school

- **Transform your city or village experience adding beauty,** like Zaandam in the Netherlands did with water and Dutch architecture buildings, and Valogno in Italy did with murals all around the village.

2. EXPERIENCE AND PRESERVE NATURE

Well, we can't quite make you experience nature with our book – unless you are reading our book somewhere outdoors (which we hope you are doing). However, since science says that what you imagine to be happening is actually happening as far as your brain is concerned, we'll use images in this second part too, trusting that visualization will be a good surrogate to experience nature. For our nature category, our lead Yellow Goldfish example is

#4. FARMCAMPS AND KIDS' PASSPORT

Farmcamps is all about adventurous farm holidays and spending time in nature. Founders believe that understanding farming should be part of a child's education, and they recognize that they can help create future agricultural entrepreneurs with good Farmcamps experiences.

Photo credit: Rosaria Cirillo Louwman

Yellow Goldfish – "BoerenPassport."[103] This farmer's passport for kids fosters education and learning through adventure. When arriving in a Farmcamps, kids receive a special EU passport from the Kingdom of "Farmer Adventures." During their stay, kids get stamps for each activity completed (remember the value of gamification from chapter 9?), and they can also see all the activities available at all the different Farmcamps, encouraging more Farmcamps experiences at other locations to complete the passport.

#5. KOKETT PACKAGING TURNS EVERY NOSE-BLOWING INTO A HOLIDAY FEELING

Photo credit: Rosaria Cirillo Louwman

According to science, visualizing a holiday place can make you feel as if you are on holiday and release dopamine in your body.

One of the things that we often look at multiple times a day, especially in cold and flu or allergy seasons, are tissues' packages. Yet 95 percent of the boxes on the market only have a boring brand name/logo on their packaging.

Kokett's Yellow Goldfish is to take away dull and have colorful packaging featuring beautiful sea and tropical island images.

---

103 www.farmcamps.nl/boerenpaspoort.html

#6. AH "MOESTUINJE" PROMOTION

For four consecutive years, Albert Hein (a major supermarket chain in the Netherlands) has run a customer loyalty promotion called "*Moestuintje.*" (Little vegetable garden). For each 10€ purchase, you receive a small paper box that includes seeds and soil to mix to plant in your garden or small planter in your home. These little boxes contribute to customer happiness by creating a beautiful experience that children can share with their parents and by fostering learning moments for the children and pride when the seeds blossom into vegetables or fruit a few months later. For families who do have a garden, the small boxes provide a stimulus for the kids to spend time outdoors to plant their seeds and later to water their plants and see them grow and blossom, as we will see in chapter 23.

Photo credit: Rosaria Cirillo Louwman

ADDITIONAL WAYS TO EXPERIENCE AND PRESERVE NATURE

- **Embrace Circular Economy** by respecting, restoring, and regenerating resources like Dopper, Innocent, Timberland, and RAW do.
- **Grow a garden** for employees at work to cultivate vegetables, as Promega did.
- **Add plants and colors** to your city to make it more joyful[104], as Urban Happiness studies suggest[105].
- **Add nature** even in the middle of traffic, as Mexico did.

The "N" in H.A.P.P.I.N.E.S.S. stands for Nature. Let's move on to the E.

104 www.theconversation.com/look-up-happycity-and-heres-what-youll-find-97248
105 www.researchgate.net/publication/322777034_Images_of_Urban_Happiness_A_Pilot_Study_in_the_Self-representation_of_Happiness_in_Urban_Spaces

CHAPTER 12

EMPATHY

"Empathy is the skill or ability to tap into our own experiences in order to connect with an experience someone is relating to us."

–Brené Brown

THIS CHAPTER IN FIVE SENSES

- Art
- Daffodil
- Song: *Need you now* (Lady Antebellum)
- Chocolate
- Silk

TEDx Talk:
The Power of Vulnerability | Brené Brown

THE "E" IN H.A.P.P.I.N.E.S.S. STANDS FOR EMPATHY.

When we share a problem or worry we have with someone who minimizes it in response, we immediately feel sadness, at times, even fear, shame, or anger. On the other hand, when we share the same problem or worry with someone who sees how we are experiencing the world, acknowledges how we feel, and expresses that back to us, we immediately feel accepted, connected, relieved, and ultimately a little happier than before we shared our issue. We expand. Why is it that?

Let's look at what science, psychology, and chemistry have to say.

SCIENCE AND RESEARCH

The latest research in neuroscience has revealed that we have what scientists call "*social brain,*" a region that lights up when we are engaged in social interactions. Matthew Lieberman, a social cognitive neuroscientist, writes: "This network comes on like a reflex, and it directs us to think about other people's minds, their thoughts, feelings, and goals. It promotes understanding, **empathy**, **cooperation,** and **consideration**."

Lieberman set-up a neuroimaging study using functional magnetic resonance imaging (fMRI) while people performed a psychological test called the "prisoner's dilemma." The fMRI results showed that a participant's reward center was more sensitive to the total amount earned by both players than to their personal outcome. This result means that **people got more pleasure from the happiness of others than from their own happiness**.

From an evolutionary standpoint, empathy is a valuable impulse that helped us survive in groups. Humans could not have survived without compassion and solidarity. We are all wired for empathy; we just have to learn how to connect the wires to make it work.[106]

In his book *Social Intelligence: The New Science of Human Relationships*, Daniel Goleman shows how the latest findings in biology and neuroscience confirm that we are wired for connection and that our relationships shape our biology as well as our experiences.

Goleman writes, "Even our most routine encounters act as regulators in the brain, priming our emotions, some desirable, others not. The more strongly connected we are with someone emotionally, the greater the mutual force."

And feeling connected to other people is at the heart of happiness. All existing research on happiness confirms that the quality of relationship with the people we care about and surround ourselves with is the number one predictor of Happiness. Not only that, but research also shows that people with strong social relationships live longer lives.[107]

PSYCHOLOGY

We include under the "EMPATHY, BELONGING, AND CONNECTION" category the following universal human needs:

- Acceptance / Inclusion
- Appreciation
- Care/Kindness
- Closeness

106 *The Danish Way of Parenting*, by Jessica Joelle Alexander and Iben Dissing Sandahl
107 Source: Peterson 2013, Pursuing the Good Life, Oxford University Press

- Communication
- Community
- Compassion
- Consideration
- Cooperation
- Love
- Mutuality
- Nurturing
- Reassurance
- Sharing/Giving
- Support
- Understanding
- Trust

CHEMISTRY

From a chemical point of view, connection makes us happy because we produce oxytocin (the "Bonding Molecule") as a result of interactions with others and, in turn, stimulates behaviors that enable social bonding such as eye contact, social recognition, and trust.

In her book *10 Keys to Happier Living*, Vanessa King explains that "oxytocin calms our fears, making us more willing to connect and display gestures of friendliness, which, in turn, increase oxytocin in the other person, triggering a spiral of mutual connection, responsiveness, and care."

In business, more oxytocin equals:

- more opportunities to create trust in a sales scenario (and make the sale happen)
- more opportunities to solve customer service enquires or problems without them escalating into stressful (and often lengthy and unsuccessful) interactions.
- happier and healthier employees

EMPATHY AND CONNECTION IN BUSINESS

In business, one of the most frequent opportunities (or threats) for connection is Customer Service Interactions. These interactions are most often very emotion-rich for customers and, as a consequence, for employees too.

When interacting with humans, customers are more emotionally resonant than when their interactions are with digital touchpoints.[108] As companies embrace digital transformation, customer-facing employees will play a critical role in creating memorable experiences associated with positive emotions—or negative ones when things go wrong. Why? Because:

- **Customers use a contact center instead of self-service when problems are complicated.** Thanks to online self-service tools and chatbots, most easy queries (like the status of order delivery) never make it to a call center. The questions that do come in (like why the important delivery I was expecting yesterday hasn't

108 In Forrester's 2017 US CX index, significantly more customers who used nondigital channels to interact with brands felt positive emotions during the interaction compared to those who used only digital channels. Source: Forrester Data Customer experience index online Survey, US Consumers 2017

arrived yet) are often tricky and fraught with emotion. They can make or break the relationship with your customers.

- **Contact center interactions often happen at critical moments or high emotion times in a customer's life.** Usually, the situation necessitating a contact center call occurs around a life event such as marriage, birth, divorce, illness, or death of a loved one—an emotional time in its own right.
- **Contact center resolution can influence a customer's "remembering self."** Correct emotional response and resolution during a service interaction can make a difference in what customers remember about their experience with the company.

By enabling your employees to create positive emotional connections with your customers, you will increase both customer and employee happiness and, at the same time, reduce bottom-line costs thanks to lower attrition and more efficient and effective interactions.

Let's look at five *Yellow Goldfish* we found in this category.

#1. UPIC HEALTH PATIENT CARE

UPIC Health, a Patient Communications Center, has been growing organically six-fold for the past three years, helping clients provide empathetic care to women all over the U.S.

UPIC has been selected as a CEO Report 2018 Velocity Growth Award winner for its determination, dedication, and drive to serve its clients and employees, and reached EBITDA of 20 percent in just three years.

UPIC Health has made *Empathy* the center of their business model. CEO Mary Tucker defines empathy like this: "*We are the women we serve.*"

"Our thriving business model proves that empathetic care and healthy bottom lines are not mutually exclusive," says Tucker, who founded UPIC Health in 2014 after identifying an urgent need for value-based customer care in the healthcare industry. UPIC also reports employee turnover below 5 percent, which is extraordinary in this industry.[109]

Yellow Goldfish – meaningful partnerships: UPIC increases its employees' sense of purpose and capabilities to empathize with the customers they serve by partnering with organizations that align with both its employees' personal and UPIC corporate values. Some of these partnerships include:

- BRAWS (Bringing Resources to Aid Women's Shelters) in Fairfax and Loudoun Counties Virginia[110]
- H.E.R. Shelter (Help and Emergency Response Inc.) in Hampton Roads, Virginia[111]
- N Street Village in Washington, D.C.[112]

Juli Briskman, Chief Marketing Officer of UPIC Health, explains:

> These events help employees realize that in comparison to some in desperate need for food, shelter, feminine hygiene products, bras, and underwear, their lives are pretty good. But it also provides a window into the lives of the very clients we often serve, and that translates to our communications center daily. We are who we serve. We see ourselves in them.

---

109 www.upichealth.com/patient-communications-center/
110 www.upichealth.com/new-braws-partnership-aids-local-women-who-need-it-most/
111 A non-profit shelter that assists victims of domestic and relationship violence, stalking, and human trafficking. www.upichealth.com/upicares-partners-with-her-shelter-in-norfolk/
112 www.upichealth.com/volunteerism-continues-at-n-street-village/

UPICares recently partnered with BRAWS (Bringing Resources to Aid Women's Shelters), and the response from our team has been amazing. When we first approached the team, we shared that students in Loudoun and Fairfax Counties (Virginia) were missing school because they lacked the feminine hygiene products needed to get them through the day. The products are expensive, carry a pink tax, and families often must prioritize other necessities. The team was appalled. We are a mostly-women organization, and everyone can relate to having our periods and the threat of being exposed or embarrassed if our products do not contain the flow. As we discovered, in addition to missing school, women in shelters are missing interviews and other appointments. They are generally suffering because they cannot afford feminine hygiene products and even bras and underwear that fit well. In our view, this is demoralizing and speaks to the overall inequity in society.

We have since held a drive for BRAWS, attended their 5K event to raise money, and attended a distribution event. UPICares also has organized a donation/fundraising event in D.C. and will continue to work with BRAWS as our missions are so closely aligned.

#2. LEXUS OMOTENASHI

Omotenashi is the Japanese spirit of hospitality that anticipates and fulfills people's needs. Empathy (together with anticipation and authenticity) is the core element of *omotenashi*.

Omotenashi is grounded in mutual respect and consideration for the person, such as the respect that a customer or guest shows by spending his or her time at your place of business over others. It extends beyond the "customer is always right" philosophy. It places you in your customer's shoes—ensuring customer expectations are met by building the services and products from their perspective and requiring them to exert as little effort as possible to obtain your product or service.[113]

The Lexus brand has a strong influence from Japanese *omotenashi* in every aspect of its business. Lexus dealers always treat customers as they would a guest in their own home, going to any lengths to solve their automotive problems, mechanical or otherwise. True to the concept of *omotenashi,* Lexus endeavors to do more than simply meet a person's needs and desires. They anticipate them and seamlessly deliver on that promise, so that whatever is required is always immediately available.[114]

Yellow Goldfish – Special celebration also for a second-hand car purchase. Danny Peters, CEO of Milkymap, shared how impressed he was and how it significantly contributed to his happiness, the memorable ceremony that Louwman Parqui, a Lexus dealer in the Netherlands, organized for him, even though he was purchasing a second-hand car from them, rather than a new one. Parqui transformed the car delivery moment into a truly memorable experience for Peters, an experience Peters spoke about even three years later during a CXPA networking event in June 2017 in the Netherlands. Rosaria heard him talk about the experience, saw his photos, and even a year later, remembers the telling of his experience.

During the same CXPA event, Lex van Den Elsen, Louwman Ambassador for Lexus in the Netherlands, shared more about Lexus and their brand shift from "Art of Perfection" to "Experience Amazing." Lexus listened to their customer perceptions of a boring

---

113 www.genesys.com/blog/post/omotenashi-the-japanese-art-of-exceptional-experiences
114 www.blog.lexus.co.uk/omotenashi-mean-lexus/

brand and transformed their perception by focusing on customer emotions. They changed their car goal from "transporting people" to "transporting all our senses." They turned function into emotion, performance into passion, and technology into imagination, and they fully embraced *omotenashi* as their guiding principle to create world-class CX and an "Experience Amazing" event for their customers.

#3. KPN NEXT OF KIN SUPPORT DESK

KPN is one of the leading Dutch telecom providers that also offers Internet, TV, and mobile services. Thanks to a dedicated Customer Experience Team and a focus on identifying customer experience improvements, they recognized that high call volume and cancellations were happening during critical life-changing events such as the death of a family member. "Next of kin" were calling after a death in the family to close those no-longer-needed service accounts and eliminate costs. These calls were often emotional, especially with the KPN processes and procedures not yet being up to the task. Customers were required to place separate calls for different products, send the "death certificate" by actual mail, and in some cases, were required to go to the store. These calls caused both substantial negative emotion storage in customer memory and unnecessary activity loads for the contact center.

Through a project using Design Thinking methodology, one central dedicated "*nabestaande desk*" (Next of Kin desk) was set-up. In the HOW of the book, we will look more into the set-up on this. For the moment, we simply want to share their Yellow Goldfish.

Yellow Goldfish - recording of the voicemail welcome message of the deceased: KPN now also offers the opportunity to send the next of kin the recording of the welcome voicemail message of their deceased family member. The "next of kin" employee can make this offer this during a phone call based on an assessment of whether this will be appreciated. Especially for elderly customers, this might be the only voice recording available, so family members may find it heart-warming to receive this lasting memory of their loved one.

Susan Oudshoorn, the CX Lead, shared with us, "In one case, we got a special thank-you. A woman mailed to let us know that the recording of her deceased mother's voicemail contained the voice of her sister that passed away a few months earlier. This unexpected content made it even more special and impactful. The colleagues of the next of kin desk are genuinely grateful to be able to offer this 'gift' that makes for a pleasant surprise in a very emotional time."

#4. BROOKINGS TWIST TO BRING KIDS TO WORK

"Take Our Kids to Work Day" is a great initiative that is being implemented by many companies. Some examples in the Netherlands are Philips, Albelli, and Simyo. This kind of program allows for more family connection and sharing. It also creates a more profound sense of belonging for the employees.

For this category, we found a company that has gone a step further in making this initiative inclusive and impactful.

Yellow Goldfish - Take Our Daughters and Sons to Work Day: The Brookings Institution does this program with a twist: Employee's take someone else's kid to work instead of their own.

Richard V. Reeves, a Senior Fellow at The Brookings Institution, says[115]:

> Take Our Daughters and Sons to Work Day is intended to get children thinking about their future careers, but by having parents take their kids to work, we perpetuate class

115 www.brookings.edu/opinions/theres-a-better-way-to-celebrate-take-your-kids-to-work-day-taking-someone-elses-kid-instead/

> divides. If your mother is a lawyer, you spend the day in a law firm. If your dad stocks shelves in a grocery store, then—if he is even allowed to bring you along—that's what you will see. If your parents are unemployed, you don't have a chance to go anywhere at all. And so the wheel turns.
>
> At Brookings, we are trying to practice what we preach. So this Friday, we will be hosting over 100 high schoolers from DC Public Schools as a result of a new partnership with two non-profit organizations—Build DC and the Latin American Youth Center—and DC Public Schools.

#5. "STEP BY STEP PROGRAM" IN THE DANISH SCHOOL SYSTEM

In *The Danish Way of Parenting*, Jessica Joelle Alexander and Iben Dissing Sandahl share this best practice:

> In the Danish school system, there is a mandatory national program implemented as early as preschool called ***Step by Step***. The children are shown pictures of kids, each exhibiting a different emotion: sadness, fear, anger, frustration, happiness, and so on. The kids talk about these cards and put into words what the child is sensing, learning to conceptualize their own, and others' feelings. They learn empathy, problem-solving, self-control, and how to read facial expressions. The facilitators and children aren't judgmental of the emotions they see. Instead, they simply recognize and respect them. Since empathy is one of the single most important factors in making successful leaders, entrepreneurs, managers, and businesses, if we focus on actively teaching empathy to our children (as they do in

Denmark), we can create the opportunity for happier adults in the future.

ADDITIONAL WAYS TO INCREASE EMPATHY

- **Encourage employees to practice "Loving Kindness" meditation.** Also called "metta," this form of meditation increases our capacity to self-generate positive emotions by focusing on compassion for self and others.
- **Allow employees to create high-quality connections and relationships with one another**. Relationship building has both physical and emotional benefits, like enhanced cardio and immune responses. Eli Lilly and Company has created numerous affinity groups to increase multi-cultural competency and an inclusive environment in which relationships between all co-workers can form.[116]
- **Create heartwarming commercials** that represent life in customers' real shoes and promote a better world, like Nike, WestJet, BBQ Quebec, and Income did.

The "E" in H.A.P.P.I.N.E.S.S. stands for Empathy. Let's move on to the first S.

---

116 www.positiveorgs.bus.umich.edu/wp-content/uploads/ItsTheLittleThingsThatMatter.pdf

CHAPTER 13

SIMPLICITY

"Perfection is achieved not when there is nothing more to add,

but when there is nothing left to take away."

– Antoine de Saint-Exupery

THIS CHAPTER IN FIVE SENSES

- Mountain Views
- Dahlia
- Song: *Simple* (Florida Georgia Line)
- Cheese
- Dough

TEDx Talk:
Simplicity Sells | David Pogue

THE FIRST "S" IN H.A.P.P.I.N.E.S.S. STANDS FOR SIMPLICITY.

The quote about simplicity by french writer Antoine de Saint-Exupery's is a great reminder that often less is more—or at least better. Whether you're a designer, writer, or anything else, many of us tend toward too much detail when we should be erring on the side of simplicity. The more you can cut, the more efficient you can be in conveying your message or designing an experience that creates happiness.

The key to simplicity is the concept of "just the right amount": finding the middle ground to satisfy customer, employee, or societal needs. Ted Bauer calls this the *Goldilocks effect*:[117]

> **Companies with too many rules** tended to "hit the mark" — i.e., release a product — but it tended to be the wrong thing relative to what everyone wanted. Logically, you'd assume the process (too many rules) made it so they weren't even solving the right problem (or needs).
>
> **Companies with no real rules** tended to get nothing done — no outcomes or deliverables. That's not good, although I bet those companies did achieve a whole bunch of no-ROI deliverables.
>
> **Companies in the middle — 4 or 5 simple rules** — tended to achieve the most.
>
> So, there's a sweet spot for simplicity in business: 4 or 5 simple rules that guide process and protocol, but not 14 or 15 (overwhelming) and not 0 or 1 (everyone's slacking off).

117 www.thecontextofthings.com/2016/04/04/simplicity-in-business/

Less is more. According to Tim Nash, "We have enough complexity in our lives already. No one is looking to increase it." We need to remember the K.I.S.S. method (keep it short and simple).

PSYCHOLOGY

We include under the "SIMPLICITY & ORDER" category the following universal human needs:

- Awareness
- Clarity/Direction
- Education/Learning
- Efficiency
- Focus
- Information
- Structure

Let's look at four *Yellow Goldfish* we found in this category.

#1. T-MOBILE SIMPLIFIES CUSTOMER SERVICE FOR FAMILY MEMBERS AND FRIENDS

In 2014, T-Mobile set out to stimulate ambassadorship among its employees in the Netherlands. They wanted a simple way to empower employees with the ability to address questions or complaints in real-time. The answer was a mobile application.

Yellow Goldfish - NL CEO App: In 2015, T-Mobile NL launched the CEO app. The app enables everyone in the company to submit a ticket to customer service. According to Mischa van Gelderen, CEO stands for Customer Experience Officer. Here's what the employees can do with the CEO app:

- They can help family, friends, and relatives by quickly solving T-Mobile related questions/complaints. Within 48 hours, the question/complaint will be answered directly to the family, friend, or relative.
- It enables employees to give benefits to customers, like a one-time discount on the next invoice. The customer gets a personalized (with the name of the employee) SMS that he or she will receive a benefit. Each employee received 15 credits at the launch of the CEO app. When they give away a gift, the credit is deducted from their balance. Employees can earn additional credits by listening to customers while helping the web care team, listening at customer service, or joining the courier when delivering the mobile phone or sim card at the customer's home.
- They can find a colleague and share knowledge, give compliments, and see event announcements.

In 2017, the almost 2,000 Customer Experience officers had a busy year. Through the CEO app, more than 48,000 benefits were given, more than 5,000 new customers were gained, almost 2,000 problems were resolved, and about 40,000 colleagues were "located." Now three years after the launch of the CEO app, nearly every T-Mobile employee has the app on his/her device and uses it daily.

#2. HEADSPACE AND MEDITATION

Andy Puddicombe is a meditation and mindfulness expert. In his early twenties, midway through college, Andy made the unexpected decision to travel to the Himalayas to study meditation instead. It was the beginning of a ten-year journey that took him around the world, culminating with ordination as a Tibetan Buddhist monk in Northern India. His transition back to lay life in 2004 was no less extraordinary.

Training briefly at *Moscow State Circus*, he returned to London where he completed a degree in Circus Arts with the *Conservatoire of Dance and Drama*, while drawing up the early plans for what was later to become Headspace.[118] Founded in 2012, Headspace is a digital health company that provides guided meditation training and mindfulness for its users. Puddicombe co-founded the company with Rich Pierson. They aimed to simplify the complex and demystify meditation. They sought to make it more accessible, more relevant to the modern-day world, and more creatively engaging.[119]

Yellow Goldfish - Headspace app: The strength of Headspace is the simplicity of its app. All of the meditations have the same voice as founder Andy Puddicombe. Each pack of meditations contains thematic singles which allow you to meditate in every possible situation (walking, cycling, or even doing house-cores) or mood. Users can also choose the length of each meditation to fit their exact needs. Rosaria uses the app regularly when taking a nature walk or when taking breaks from writing.

#3. WD-40 AND FOCUS ON ENGAGEMENT

WD-40 Company is one of the world's most recognizable brands. It enjoys a high level of employee engagement. An astounding 98 percent of employees say they "love to work" at the company. This increased engagement has resulted in sustained growth. WD-40 has doubled in revenue in the last decade and is on a trajectory to double again in the next. CEO Garry Ridge believes the growth is a byproduct of the engagement.[120]

Yellow Goldfish – Versatility: WD-40's fantastic versatility is why you'll find a can in every home and workshop. Their focus is to

---

118 www.headspace.com/andy-puddicombe
119 www.en.wikipedia.org/wiki/Andy_Puddicombe
120 www.positivesharing.com/2018/06/how-wd-40-built-a-billion-dollar-business-with-happiness/

"Make your customers look awesome, not your products." WD-40 focuses on celebrating all the great things customers do with the product. In fact, their company purpose says nothing at all about their products: We create positive lasting memories by solving problems in workshops, factories, and homes around the world. A prominent section on their website showcases how customers have used their products to solve various issues, including things like:

- displacing moisture from your jet ski spark plugs
- removing crayon stains
- removing a python that was coiled around the undercarriage of a bus (in Asia)

If you have discovered an excellent use for their products (over 2,000 benefits exist), you can submit it and get yourself featured on their website[121]. This approach works: WD-40 has a fan club with 125,000 members. Does your product or company make people so happy that they form fan clubs in your honor?

#4. APPLE AND SIMPLICITY

Steve Jobs met Steve Wozniak at the Homebrew Computer Club, a gathering of enthusiasts in a garage in California's Menlo Park. Wozniak had seen his first MITS Altair there and was inspired by the build-it-yourself approach of the Altair kit to make something more straightforward for the rest of us. So, he produced the first computer with a typewriter-like keyboard and the ability to connect to a regular TV. Later christened the Apple I, it would become the archetype of the modern computer. This drive to simplify would become the hallmark of the brand. "It takes a lot of hard work," Steve Jobs said,

---

121 www.wd40.com/uses-tips

"to make something simple, to truly understand the underlying challenges and come up with elegant solutions." As the headline of Apple's first marketing brochure proclaimed in 1977, "Simplicity is the ultimate sophistication."

Yellow Goldfish – iPod, iPhone, and iPad: Jobs' belief in the power of simplicity as a design precept reached its pinnacle with the three consumer device triumphs he produced beginning in 2001: the iPod, iPhone, and iPad. He immersed himself daily in the design of the original iPod and its interface. His primary demand was "Simplify!" He would go over each screen and apply a rigorous test: If he wanted a song or a function, he should be able to get there in three clicks. And the clicks should be intuitive. This focus on simplicity had driven the company to a trillion-dollar valuation in 2018. Apple CEO Tim Cook said that market capitalization was "not the most important measure" of the company's success but was instead a result of its focus on its products, customers, and company values.[122]

Alas, as we write this update in August 2020, the iOS updated for the past two years don't seem to deliver on Job's promise and surely don't pass the rigorous test of three intuitive clicks.

ADDITIONAL WAYS TO INCREASE SIMPLICITY

- **Kill a stupid rule** – We are inundated with regulations in the workplace. Rules are generally born out of reactions to past issues and sometimes remain in place even when the reasons for them cease to exist. In her book, *Kill the Company: End the Status Quo, Start an Innovation Revolution*, Lisa Bodell suggests a process called "Kill a Stupid Rule." It starts with a simple question to team members, "If you could kill or change all the stupid rules

122 www-cnbc-com.cdn.ampproject.org/c/s/www.cnbc.com/amp/2018/08/03/apple-ceo-calls-1-trillion-value-a-milestone-but-not-a-focus.html

that get in the way of doing your work or better serving our customers, what would they be, and how would you do it?" Ideas are collected, and rules are evaluated based on impact and degree of difficulty to abolish.[123]

- **Look for the pencil solution** – Sometimes, the answer to a problem may be the simplest. Decades ago, NASA allegedly spent over $1 million and 12 months to develop a pen that would write in zero gravity and low pressure. The Russians just used a pencil. According to Gordon Tredgold,[124] "We need to check to see if a pencil solution exists, and if so, then go with that."

The first "S" in H.A.P.P.I.N.E.S.S. stands for Simplicity. Let's move on to the second S.

123 www.thinkingbusinessblog.com/2015/05/28/five-simple-steps-to-kill-a-stupid-rule-and-boost-your-business/
124 www.inc.com/gordon-tredgold/3-daily-habits-to-increase-your-productivity-and-efficiency.html

CHAPTER 14

SMILE

"A smile is happiness you'll find right under your nose."

– Tom Wilson

THIS CHAPTER IN FIVE SENSES

- Fireworks
- Sunflowers
- Song: *Celebration* (Kool & The Gang)
- Champagne
- Glitter

***TEDx Talk*:**
The epidemic of smiles and the science of gratitude
Jennifer Moss

THE SECOND "S" IN H.A.P.P.I.N.E.S.S. STANDS FOR SMILE.

When we smile, or someone smiles at us (and we feel compelled to smile in return), we immediately feel better. Why is that?

When we smile, we send a message to the body to rebalance, to cultivate health, vitality, and inner joy. As you will discover in the meditation section at the end of this chapter (a little lagniappe from us to you), smiling energy is a way to cultivate gratitude, healing, and empowerment.

SCIENCE AND RESEARCH

In her TEDx Talk (2014) "The epidemic of smiles and the science of gratitude," Jennifer Moss shares the story of how she and her husband, Jim, made it through a challenging period thanks to:

- the narrative they choose to embrace.
- the daily gratitude they started practicing—even for things as simple as "Jim relearned to brush his teeth today."
- the smiles, even if they had to force themselves to smile at times.

Amy Cuddy says: "If you feel like you shouldn't be somewhere: Fake it. Do it not until you make it—but until you become it."

In Jen's words, "our smiles were literally making us fake it until we became that smile."

Science proves that there is a feedback loop in the brain so that when we smile, the joy region of the brain is activated. You either smile and are joyful, or you are cheerful, and then you smile. So, smiling will help you through until you become joyful.

We will cover further the science behind the power of a smile, celebration, and cultivating gratitude under Yellow Goldfish #1 & #2.

PSYCHOLOGY

We include under the "SMILE and CELEBRATION" category the following universal human needs:

- Acknowledgment
- Award
- Celebration of dreams fulfilled
- Celebration of life
- Expressing & receiving gratitude
- Mourning losses
- Recognition
- Reward

CHEMISTRY

From a chemical point of view, this category gives us a complete DOSE of H.A.P.P.I.N.E.S.S. by activating all of our happiness chemicals. DOSE examples include:

- celebrating and presenting an award, which makes us happy because it releases **D**opamine. ("The Reward Molecule")
- giving an award during a public award ceremony where there are authentic handshakes or hugs and chance to connect, or occasions for singing or performing together. These activities make us additionally happy because they release **O**xytocin. ("The Bonding Molecule")
- practicing gratitude and increasing awareness for ways to pursue things that reinforce a sense of purpose, meaning, and

accomplishment, or even recalling happy memories which releases **S**erotonin. ("The Confidence Molecule")

- smiling, which makes us happy because when we smile or laugh, we produce **E**ndorphin ("The Pain-Killing Molecule"), and we forget all of our pain and sorrows!

SMILE & CELEBRATION IN BUSINESS

Here are some opportunities for smiles, celebrations, and gratitude in business:

- Take the time and make an effort to demonstrate and promote an appreciation for employees, teams, colleagues, and customers in the workplace, verbally, in writing, and in ordinary and milestone celebrations
- Create and enable reward opportunities throughout the company
- Organize award events to recognize, celebrate, congratulate, and show gratitude
- Offer employee perks and benefits that resonate with the part of your company culture that attracts employees and customers to your company

GRATITUDE AND PROFITABILITY

Gratitude has powerful and lasting impacts on productivity. Plasticity Labs Research[125] suggests that:

---

125 White Paper on benefits of Gratitude: www.plasticitylabs.com/wp-content/uploads/2017/01/Gratitude-At-Work-White-Paper.pdf

- Grateful people are better at perspective-taking and are more agreeable and more open to new ideas, all of which have important implications for the workplace.
- Gratitude promotes prosocial behavior, which can contribute to social support and cohesiveness among team members with an increased sense of community—a fantastic byproduct for employers looking for ways to increase engagement.
- There is a correlation between gratitude and decreased procrastination, which is good for productivity.

The study proved that employees who focused on and described three things that they were thankful for at work reported more workplace-specific gratitude. Employees who also write them down before the start of every workday increase the likelihood of promotions by 40%; improve sales by 35%; reduce coding errors by 37%, and even enhance healthiness by reducing sick days from six to two every year.

According to Dr. Robert Emmons, the foremost researcher in gratitude and its impact on performance, people who spent ten weeks writing down weekly gratitude statements felt 25% happier; they were more optimistic about the future; they felt better about their lives, and they exercised almost 1.5 hours more per week than people who, conversely, shared their weekly hassles.[126]

Rewarding employees with unique benefits and perks is also a great way to contribute to employee happiness and generate more smiles while increasing profitability by reducing employee's turnover and burnout rate. This outcome is especially true when the perks are about lifetime experiences.

---

126 www.skipprichard.com/how-to-unlock-happiness-at-work/

Let's look at five *Yellow Goldfish* we found in this category.

#1. PLASTICITY AND GRATITUDE

Plasticity is a mission-driven technology and consulting company committed to giving one billion people the tools to live a happier, healthier, and high performing life.

Plasticity Co-founder Jim Moss was a Hall of Fame, gold medal-winning, a pro athlete. But in the weeks leading up to the 2009 season, he was suddenly rendered acutely paralyzed from a rare autoimmune disease.

As an athlete of this caliber, he knew what it would take to fight his way back, but the doctors weren't sure how long it would take to walk again. Ignoring the naysayers, Jim hacked his own healing and focused on being grateful and learning the science of mood and performance. He walked out of the hospital six weeks later.[127]

During this year's World Happiness Festival in Mexico, Jennifer Moss shared a story that much touched Rosaria and stayed with her. During his rehab hospital stay, Jim, who had a powerful desire to compete and win, would refuse to stay in bed and use a bedpan and preferred instead to take a slow and painful walk to the bathroom, with a 10-step break between him and the goal. The nurses who were eager to get back to work would have to wait patiently for Jim. Jennifer shared this account:

> One morning, with annoyance at this time-consuming effort, the **morning nurse** told Jim that he "*better get used to it, you're going to be like this for a long time!*"
>
> This wholly gutted Jim. When I saw him later, his demotivation could be felt on his face and throughout his

127 www.plasticitylabs.com/about-us/

> sluggish body. This comment would haunt Jim. But it would also motivate him.
>
> In the evening, he got back up and initiated the excruciatingly slow walk to the bathroom. But this time, as Jim took his regular 10-step break between him and the goal, the **evening nurse** said jovially, "*Don't you worry about it, sweetheart, you'll get back on your feet in no time.*"
>
> These are the defining moments of our lives. They break us — or they advance us.[128]

Jennifer closed her talk with the question that we would like to share with you: "*Who do you want to be, the morning nurse or the evening nurse?*"

This life experience taught Jim and Jen that mood drives performance, and that we can influence our brain and our body. Our daily habits impact our mood and subsequently make us who we are. The term ***neuroplasticity*** comes from the root words **neuron** and **plastic**. It refers to the **brain's ability** to reorganize by creating new neural pathways to adapt as needed. Hence our experiences change both the brain's physical structure (anatomy) and functional organization (physiology).

And this experience was the catalyst for Jim and Jen to start Plasticity Labs, a research and technology company that increases psychological fitness for individuals so they can better handle stress and trauma.

Plasticity Labs is a class-leading, award-winning technology and consulting company focused on building happier, healthier

---

128 This story is also online on www.skipprichard.com/how-to-unlock-happiness-at-work/ and in Jennifer Moss book *Unlocking Happiness at Work*

workplaces. Plasticity has the most extensive and longest-running database of employee happiness and factors impacting culture and well-being in the workplace.

Recognized by *Canadian Business* as Innovators of the Year for 2018, Plasticity is one of Canada's latest success stories and quickly becoming a leader in people analytics and HR technology. Co-founder and CCO Jennifer Moss is a founding member of the United Nation's Global Happiness Council for The Council of Workplace Happiness and contributor to the 2018 Global Happiness Report.[129]

Yellow Goldfish - Gratitude Guinness World Record: While Jim was in the hospital, Jen and Jim started looking for reasons to smile. The practice continued even when they were back home with a family "gratitude moment" at dinner. They noticed that simply asking their kids to report on things that made them grateful during the day made their son not only build a language to express gratitude but also pay more attention during the day to something to be thankful for. Jen and Jim decided to start sharing this gratitude practice online and created a website "The Smiles Epidemic"[130]— because smiles are contagious—to share what they were grateful for. People started smiling back and share their reasons to be thankful.

Fast forward a few years, and to celebrate the UN's International Day of Happiness on March 20, 2018, Plasticity set out to build the world's biggest gratitude wall, inviting everyone to be part of making happiness history by posting their gratitude note on the wall. Customers, employees, local citizens, and pretty much the entire world was offered the opportunity to submit their gratitude statement via social media and the Plasticity Facebook page. Beginning March 1st, hundreds of people tweeted their gratitude message to Plasticity

---

129 www.plasticitylabs.com/about-us/
130 www.thesmileepidemic.tumblr.com/

or posted their three reasons to be grateful on Facebook or LinkedIn. Those messages were transcribed to a sticky note for the wall.[131]

Plasticity's goal was to have 5,000 sticky notes with gratitude messages up on the wall by 6 p.m. that Tuesday in the presence of three Guinness World Record witnesses. The record to break was 2,500 messages. Plasticity exceeded their 5,000-message goal with a record-setting 6,115 gratitude notes.

Photo credit: Jennifer Moss and Luke-Sarazin

#2. AEGON

Aegon is a worldwide life insurance and pension company, operating in twenty countries and having approximately 28,000 employees. Aegon's purpose is "***helping people achieve a lifetime of financial security.***" They used to be a company very numbers and products driven. Then they embraced not only a focus shift to customer-centricity but also made a real paradigm shift to "a life event company." Under the leadership of CEO Alex Wynaendts, Aegon

131 www.cbc.ca/news/canada/kitchener-waterloo/gratitude-wall-plasticity-kitchener-tannery-1.4580029

started its transformation process from a product-focused company into a customer-driven, digitally-enabled service company. Rien Brus, global VP of Customer Strategy, led many customer-oriented global projects.

Yellow Goldfish - GLOBAL AEGON AWARDS (GAA): The Global Aegon Awards bring the company together to celebrate the people who are making a difference across the company. In March 2018, the GAA reached its 3rd edition.

Every winner or winning team in eight awards categories receives a hand-crafted artwork and 5,000€ to spend **on an experience of a lifetime**, except for the One Aegon Award winners. Only a business unit can win this award. The winning division will receive 50,000€ to be spent on a project in their own unit.

CEO Alex Wynaendts says that one of his favorite things about the event is "*the opportunity to share my pride about what we have achieved together.*" He adds: "Sharing is critical to our success. We need to learn from each other, we need to innovate, and we need to change faster. We have people from many different countries here today. Such a diverse group is going to lead to fantastic ideas, and we should only encourage that."[132]

Just like the "gratitude at dinner moment" example (described in the Plasticity story) creates a habit to start noticing opportunities to be grateful, so initiatives like the Global Aegon Awards make employees start seeing the contributions they can make and cataloging the ones already made. And it makes them look for opportunities to contribute even more. When employees are given a chance to speak about their innovative contributions at their annual awards, they can celebrate what they accomplished, share it with their peers to multiply the learning and feel pride in fulfilling their sense

---

132 Source: 2017 Global Aegon Awards presentation

of purpose. As a result, they are motivated to keep pursuing more ways to contribute.

Finally, the event itself becomes an experience that contributes to employee happiness and fosters engagement with the company and among each other. Indeed, this ceremony is turned into a big international event where all the finalist teams from all participating countries are invited to join in person at the Aegon Headquarters for a *gezellig* event.[133] The event embraces all five senses with music, a dance performance by the Netherlands Dance Theater (NDT), food, sight, and touch; it is also live-streamed to company units in many countries, broadening the audience for this truly global event.

#3. QUALTRICS "DREAM EXPERIENCE" EVERY YEAR

Qualtrics offers its 1,700 employees a chance to fulfill a personal dream. This new benefit is for full-time employees who have been at the company for at least one year. The Utah-based company rolled out the latest bonus to its employees in January 2018 in place of the $1,500 bonus it used to give at Christmas. Qualtrics leaders started the benefit to encourage people to fulfill their dreams instead of spending their Christmas money on more mundane items, such as bills. Unused bonus money does not accumulate, as the company wants to encourage employees to savor life. 668 Qualtrics employees took advantage of the experience bonus just in the first five months.

Shaunda Zilich, Qualtrics Global Talent Brand Manager, says:[134]

> One of the best things about working for an "experience management" company is the belief in the power of experiences to shape us as employees and as people. This

---

133 You can get a glimpse of 2018 edition in YouTube video "The Global Aegon Awards 2018" on www.youtu.be/pH5EYbqrQsY

134 www.qualtrics.com/blog/experience-everything-qualtrics/

> year, we introduced a new benefit to encourage employees to explore new experiences—ideally those they have only dreamed about having.
>
> The benefit is called an "experience bonus." It is $1,500 for all employees who have worked at the company for longer than a year. It should be used to fund a 'dream'—something you would not otherwise try on your own. Qualtrics employees have already used it for experiences ranging from taking their families to Disney World to building orphanages in the Philippines and more.
>
> It is a unique benefit, according to a recently released SHRM (Society for Human Resource Management) article that encourages employees to "savor life" and follow dreams.

Qualtrics also supports the experiences that are a part of an employee's everyday life with other benefits such as a '*Work Hard/Play Harder'* mentality. "For every bit of hard work we put in, we have twice the fun," they say. Qualtricians always find ways to "play" in their surroundings, whether that means taking a break in a massage chair, hitting the slopes after work, throwing a frisbee with "man's best friend" in the garden at Provo, enjoying Seattle's rooftop patio overlooking the Puget Sound, or grabbing a beer in the Dublin office pub. The latter is a perk that also Rosaria had the chance to enjoy when setting up Qualtrics for one of her clients, but only after completing the set-up, checking out their ping-pong table, and grabbing a book from their reading library too. And Qualtrics makes sure that employees take time to recharge and live it up.[135]

And for the customers? Well, they make sure their annual CX Summit is always genuinely spectacular and memorable, not only

---

135 Adapted from www.qualtrics.com/blog/experience-everything-qualtrics/

having a day for skiing or other fun activities, but also featuring special guests and outstanding performances from singers or bands such as Sir Elton John, Journey, Aerosmith, and Maroon 5.

#4. HELLOFRESH NL IN-BOX SURPRISES FOR *GEZELLIG* FAMILY MOMENTS TOGETHER

HelloFresh is one of the earlier companies in the meal-kit subscription industry. While their service also contributes to happiness by providing with simplicity everything ready for three or five meals a week, their *Yellow Factor* is that they celebrate special moments across the year by adding in their boxes unexpected gifts linked to specific seasonal or country celebration:

- they added a bag of Sunflowers seeds to celebrate Mother's Day (which is also a *Yellow Factor* in the category Nature, allowing parents and kids to spend time outdoors together planting the seeds and then seeing them growing into flowers);
- they added *pannenkoekenmix* (a unique bloom mix) for "Nationale Pannenkoekendag," *kruidnotenmix* for *pepernoten* (a typical Dutch cookie) for Sinterklaas' celebration (which is quite likely the most gezellig celebration and comprehensive family moment in NL), and a mix for carrot muffins for Easter (which prompts parents and kids to spend time together first mixing, then baking, and then eating the results!)

Lagniappe for you: you can find the receipts to make Dutch pepernoten here: www.blog.hellofresh.be/zelfgemaakte-kruidnoten/

#5. 'ACTS OF KINDNESS' ART ON THE UNDERGROUND

Vanessa King mentioned this *Yellow Factor* in *10 Keys to Happier Living,* and the following details are an extract from the About page on the project website:[136]

> Acts of Kindness is a project by artist Michael Landy celebrating everyday generosity and compassion on the Tube, inviting us to notice acts of kindness, however simple and small. The artist explains, 'Sometimes we tend to assume that you have to be superhuman to be kind, rather than just an ordinary person.' So, to unsettle that idea, Acts of Kindness catches those little exchanges that are almost too fleeting and mundane to be noticed or remembered.
>
> Landy first began thinking about the idea behind Acts of Kindness immediately after making his work Break Down (Artangel, 2001). For Break Down, he destroyed all his belongings, from his birth certificate to his car. The experience of being left with nothing helped him reflect on what we are aside from what we own, and on the value of feeling part of a common humanity.

It began when Landy was in a subway train and noticed two strangers, one of whom was trying to help the other. He wondered what inspired the act, what had motivated one stranger to help another. He created The Acts of Kindness Project to capture and explore what happens in that moment of kindness, sharing that sense of connection with someone you don't know. 'It's a gesture of trust between two people,' he says. 'There's a risk in that. They may just ignore you or take it the wrong way.' It requires courage and acceptance on both sides.

---

136 www.art.tfl.gov.uk/archive/actsofkindness/about/

In 2011, passengers and staff were asked to recall moments of "kindness," generosity, and compassion, which they have experienced during London Underground journeys. Landy has been placing his selection of Acts of Kindness stories in Central line stations and trains since late July 2011.

ADDITIONAL WAYS TO INCREASE SMILE & CELEBRATION

- **Celebrate special customer milestones**: **Southwest** Captain John Charles Ritchie, a former Air Force pilot, who has been flying with Southwest for more than 22 years, had been keeping a running score of how many passengers he's flown. And when on a particular flight, he was proudly carrying his one-millionth passenger, he gave the lucky passenger a bottle of champagne and an autographed copy of her boarding pass. He also found out how much the passenger paid for her ticket and reimbursed her for her flight costs out of his own pocket.[137]
- **Create reasons for customer WOW smiles and then create a WOW Wall** with all their ecstatic letters as **CityBin** did.[138]
- **Celebrate your customers' special life events**. ***Blue Band***, a butter spread brand by **Unilever**, surprised Rosaria and delivered multiple smiles to her and her two sons by mailing (getting actual physical mail already gives a smile nowadays) a gift for each of her children for their main growth stages: a bib shortly after they were born, a plastic spoon & fork when they were four months for the first bite, a plastic plate for their first bread around ten months, and then a "lunch box" for when they turned four and needed to take their lunch to school. In the Netherlands, kids go

137 www.foxnews.com/travel/2017/05/10/southwest-pilot-surprises-one-millionth-passenger-with-gifts-cash.html
138 www.wownow.eu/my-summary-of-satmetrix-net-promoter-conference-london-2015/

to a pre-school the day after they turn four years old, and parents pack a lunch with bread… and guess what? Butter! While delivering constant smiles across the years, Unilever recruits loyal clients.

- **Stimulate your employees to start** (or end) **the day with an act of mindful gratitude**: In the contact center of Pensioenfonds Horeca en Catering (a pension fund company in the Netherlands), each employee starts the day by writing a positive experience from the previous day on a dedicated wall. This ritual serves both to celebrate the positive experience and to start the new day with a positive charge and attitude.[139]
- **Celebrate a "killed project" by turning it into a fun moment**. That's what ***Ben & Jerry's*** does with their ***Flavor Graveyard*** where a marker stone is created, and a ceremony is held to commemorate a retired Ben & Jerry's ice cream flavor. Customers can even visit the flavor graveyard to see some of their old favorites.
- **Recognize employees behind the scenes**: In ***Crowe Horwath's*** *"Pay It Forward"* program, employees mentioned by name in client surveys get an automated alert to highlight which other colleagues, particularly behind the scenes, contributed to the excellent client experience. In the year after Crowe Horwath implemented[140] Pay It Forward, it recognized 50% more employees for their efforts in delivering an exceptional client experience. Unfortunately, too few firms provide this type of consistent recognition to their employee behind the scenes.
- **Applaud the efforts** of those who have gone above and beyond in living the company's values through their work: ***Etana REDwards*** event takes place during REDfast, a two-day getaway

---

139 Source: Ellen Metaal
140 www.blog.ultimatesoftware.com/employee-experience-imperative/

for all Etana staff. The awards are made by local artists and are given out to reinforce the core values at the company: *Be Open, Know, Grow, Give, and Make it Happen.*

- **Practice the ten minutes "Inner Smile Meditation."** Lagniappe: Do yourself a favor and try this meditation by Lee Holden. You can find it in Omvana [www.play.omvana.com/energizing-meditations/inner-smile-meditation], which is a great website and mobile app for meditation and soothing music, or on YouTube www.youtu.be/9jda3VKEwxM. And since August 2020, it is also available on Spotify.

The final "S" in H.A.P.P.I.N.E.S.S. stands for Smile. Now let's examine HOW to bring your *Yellow Factor* to life...

SECTION III

GROWTH HACKING (THE HOW)

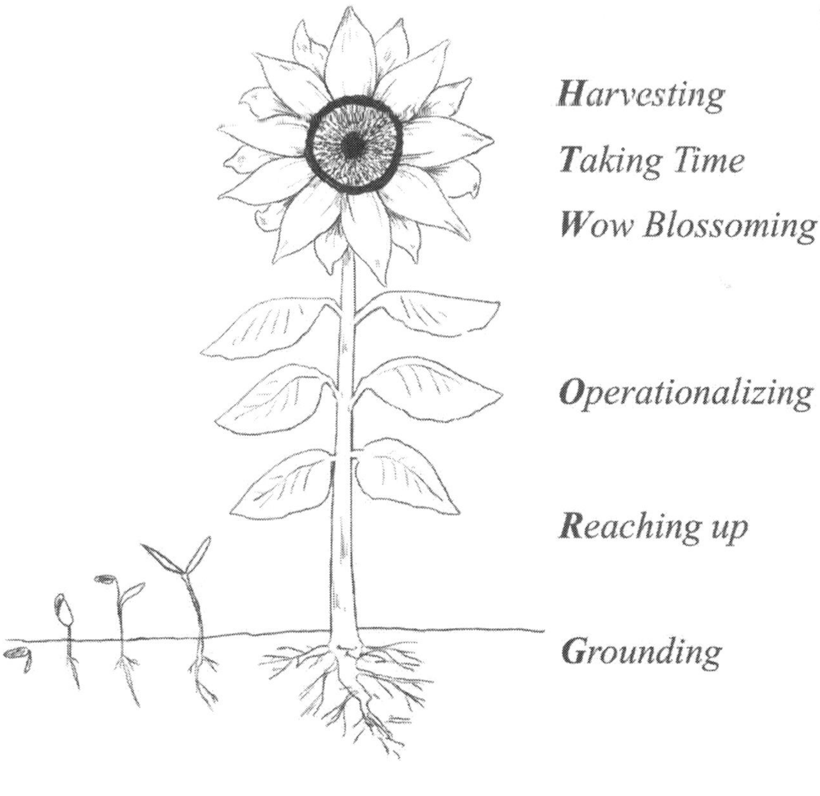

CHAPTER 15

DRIVE G.R.O.W.T.H. (CHANGE) IN SIX STEPS

"Happiness is like a seed that you need to plant, grow, and nurture with care, diligence, and time, to be able to harvest the fruits."

- Rosaria Cirillo Louwman

In the WHAT section, we have seen the nine petals of H.A.P.P.I.N.E.S.S.

In this HOW section, we cover how to nurture this HAPPINESS flower to ensure GROWTH.

In the next six chapters, we look at how you can *drive growth* and we share the process behind creating your *Yellow Factor* for Happiness Driven[141] Growth.

The process involves **G**rounding (Chapter 16), **R**eaching-up (Chapter 17), **O**perationalizing (Chapter 18), **W**ow Blossoming (Chapter 19), **T**aking Time (Chapter 20), and **H**arvesting (Chapter 21).

Inspired by the energy and warmth of yellow (the sun), the flourishing of happiness (like a flower), and the process of growth required (from seeding to blossoming), we have represented the HOW of *Yellow Factor* (GROWTH) like a… **sunflower**.

Ready to GROW? Let's start!

DRIVE G.R.O.W.T.H. (CHANGE) IN SIX STEPS

Based on the examples we have collected and the companies we analyzed, we have identified six steps to drive the change of ***Happiness Driven Growth***. They also represent the maturity stages of your company along this journey. Let's look at them:

1. **Grounding** is about
    a. **Seeding**: Identify or choose your seed and ground its growth in neuroscience, data, and insights
    b. **Germinating:** create deep roots and stay grounded during your growth

---

[141] While the "Happiness" and "Growth" elements of the model are covered in this book, the "Driven" part is covered in the *Wow Now HCX Masterclass Compendium: Your concise guide to Human-Centered and Happiness-Contributing Experience Leadership,* available on Amazon (ASIN B08NTS9TX2)

2. **Reaching-up** is about
    a. **Reframing:** challenge existing paradigms and ways of doing things
    b. **Adopting new ways of thinking, working and leading:** be open, attentive, and receptive; dare to want and contribute to a better more humane world
    c. **Empowering your team with knowledge, skills, and frameworks:** build your customer archetypes, formulate your customer needs pyramid; design your customer journey

3. **Operationalizing** is about developing and mastering six happiness competencies:
    a. **Shared understanding**: understand customer and employee needs, know who they are, how they perceive the interactions with your company, and how you can serve them in a way they can appreciate
    b. **Experience design, improvement, and innovation**: design and innovate existing experiences using Human-Centered Design approaches and methodologies
    c. **Empowerment**: provide employees and partners with space, budget, freedom, and the authority they need to deliver the right experiences
    d. **Enablement**: provide employees and partners with the resources and tools they need to deliver the right experiences
    e. **Measurement and ROI:** set metrics consistent with the desired change to quantify the quality of experiences and their link to the organization's overall metrics
    f. **Culture:** create a system of shared values and behaviors that focus employees on contributing to happiness (internally and externally)

4. **Wow blossoming** is about:

    a. **Wowing** your employees and customers with experiences that actually contribute to their Happiness

    b. **Connecting** authentically, through empathy, and **flourishing** as human beings

    c. **Acknowledging** and celebrating new *behaviors*

5. **Taking Time** to drive this change and make a difference is about:

    a. Taking time IN to feel and reflect (Brené Brown's TGIF)

    b. Taking Time OUT together as teams and across teams (Aegon)

    c. Taking time ON to do what you love (Google) and to review, to observe, and to correct (GE Example)

    d. Taking time OFF to enjoy life (Qualtrics)

    e. Taking DOWN-time for regular recharging so creativity can happen (Tal Ben-Shahar)

    f. Taking Time UP to celebrate (Aegon)

6. **Harvesting** your results is about:

    a. **Acknowledging** and celebrating the results of new behaviors

    b. **Giving back**: fostering growth expansion within your organization and outside by collecting your work's fruits, sharing your seeds, learnings, and best practices and letting others pollinate from them

Let's look at each stage one by one. The first stage is ***Grounding***.

CHAPTER 16

GROUNDING

"Attaining lasting happiness requires that we enjoy the journey on our way toward a destination we deem valuable. Happiness, therefore, is not about making it to the peak of the mountain, nor is it about climbing aimlessly around the mountain:

Happiness is the experience of climbing toward the peak."

– Tal Ben-Shahar

Grounding

Mettere Radici

Grounding starts from the two things essential to growth: Seeds (Seeding) and Roots (Germinating).

Nothing represents *potential* like a seed does. With everything it needs to blossom within it, a seed is a symbol of inner magic and wonder. As time capsules of life, seeds are precious parcels of hope and promise. They are the most complex organs plants ever produce, appearing in many shapes, sizes, and colors. In their desiccated or dormant state, they are transportable and can travel thousands of miles across oceans and continents, and they can live for thousands of years. Seeds have everything they need, not only to survive but also to grow into a plant when they encounter the right conditions.[142]

1. SEEDING

In business, **Seeding** is about fundamentals like creating a clear vision and mission, defining values, and formulating a strategy and action plan plus hiring the right employees for your company, and identifying your target customers. This stage includes thinking about your leadership role, what changes you want to drive in the world, and what values you want your company to exemplify and inspire. These fundamentals represent your **vision**, **mission,** and **values statements**.

In many companies analyzed, the "seed of change" was a visionary CEO who believes in the power of happiness to drive results and wants to make a difference in the world. UPIC CEO Mary Tucker and ZAPPOS CEO Tony Hsieh are examples of visionary leaders. In other cases, change started from a leader within the organization. For two examples, read about UPIC Health and Northwell CARE.

Part of Seeding is preparing your ground and growth plan by assessing where you are in the Happiness Driven Growth journey,

---

142 Adaptation from Project Calm article THE START OF IT ALL

planning your growth rate, and defining and detailing what you need to do to accomplish that growth. These elements represent your **strategy** and **action plan**. See the "Aegon Customer License" as an example.

The last part of Seeding is choosing your employees, your partners, and your suppliers and how you want to connect with them. Be clear about your recruitment and partnership requirements:

- recruit and hire based on attitude and alignment with the mission, design a human-centered onboarding training, and take the needed time to onboard new hires
- work with partners, clients, and suppliers who share your values and vision

Concerning the choice of partners and suppliers who can help you cultivate happiness driven growth, fortunately, the list of companies seeding happiness is growing exponentially.

Here are just three leading trailblazers in the Happiness field (more in the Additional Inspiration chapter at the end):

- Action for Happiness www.actionforhappiness.org/
- B-Corporations www.bcorporation.net/
- Delivering Happiness www.deliveringhappiness.com/

UPIC HEALTH PATIENT CARE RECRUITMENT AND ONBOARDING

We have already seen essential values upheld by the UPIC connection center when we looked at them in the Empathy Chapter in WHAT. In their recruitment phase, UPIC Health asks questions to identify what the applicant cares about, which change they want to see in the world, and how much they care about people, to make sure they recruit employees aligned with the UPIC culture and values. The UPIC onboarding training takes three weeks, covering in-depth awareness of the importance of empathy and emotional intelligence.

UPIC Professionals (they are not called "agents") working at the Patients Communication Center or PPC (they don't call it a "Contact Center"!) are selected, hired, and trained to be **caring, knowledgeable, and skilled.** They must display kindness and concern for others, be intelligent and well-informed, and certainly must have the knowledge and ability to supplement their training to perform their activities and tasks well.

These professionals are invited to reflect on what effect they will have on their callers and how what they say and do for the caller will affect the caller's perception of the UPIC client. This approach lays the right foundation for them to deliver empathic care.

NORTHWELL AND C.A.R.E CULTURAL CHANGE

A case of full culture change led by a team within the organization is the one from Northwell Health[143] , who implemented their Culture of C.A.R.E [Connectedness, Awareness, Respect, and Empathy] for their 60,000+ employees at 21 different locations. Intending to reach the 90th percentile in positive patient experience by 2020, in 2015 Northwell Health's Office of Patient and Customer Experience [OPCE] implemented a system-wide cultural transformation to reignite their commitment to higher expectations in care. They worked together with Delivering Happiness to **assess** the climate, **build** alignment from the top-down, and **implement** the change creating custom culture programs. Sven Gierlinger, Chief Experience Officer at Northwell Health, says, "We can have the most beautiful facilities, well-functioning processes, and a clean environment, but

143 www.blog.deliveringhappiness.com/northwell-health-case-study-a-culture-change-transformation-in-healthcare

we will still fail. We must strengthen our culture and accountability to focus on empathy, customer service, and communication across the entire organization."

The program aimed at

- Reigniting the passion of providers and staff so they can drive innovation and create meaningful experiences for patients and customers
- Fostering a commitment to and advocacy for C.A.R.E from the top-down, including executive leadership, their managers, and their staff

The results were very tangible[144]:

- Employee engagement increased from 45 to 85 percent over two years
- 20 percent of the company's ambulatory locations reached the top 90 percent ranking in the patient experience within eighteen months

AEGON "CUSTOMER LICENSE"

One of the many tools that Aegon uses to drive the cultural change into the organization is the "Aegon Customer License" program. Every employee who does not have any customer contact in his or her regular job needs to spend at least two and a half days every two years interacting with customers. To roll out the License Program to 300 people at the Aegon Corporate Center, Rien Brus organized a kick-off session each month with twelve people. He gave these colleagues assignments in pairs and three months to spend time with customers. He then got them back together at the headquarters to

144 Additional details can be found in the case study downloadable on www.info.deliveringhappiness.com/healthcareculturecasestudy

exchange stories and feedback, as the last step before obtaining their Aegon "Customer License." Consistently running a class with twelve people every month covered all 300 headquarter and country lead champions in two years. Countries across the globe have adopted a train-the-trainer approach and adapted locally to get everyone else on board too.

In *Management Scope* (Nov.2012), CEO Alex Wynaendts says about the Customer License:

> "What do an airplane pilot and an AEGON employee have in common? They both have to do their 'flight hours' to receive and to keep their license. For us, this means spending time with customers. We want to show our people that we, as Aegon, exist to help customers. And therefore, **all our employees must know what our customers' needs are**."

2. GERMINATING

Plants with deeper roots can survive higher temperatures and lack of rain for more extended periods because their roots can get water deeper in the soil. In business, the deeper your basis, and the more grounded your choices, the more reliable your potential growth opportunities will be.

Germinating includes two steps:

1. Develop deep roots by grounding your seed's growth in neuroscience, data, and insights coming from:

a. Psychology research and neurology studies (the WHY section)

b. Chemistry of happiness and well-being (the WHY section)

c. Examples from trailblazer and pioneer companies that are already on the path (the WHAT section)

d. Your own business. In the CX and EX space, this includes elements such as:

   - Values, Vision, Mission and Brand Promise
   - Voice of Customer (VOC): ask your customers what they think and feel about their experiences with your company
   - Voice of Employee (VOE): ask your employees what they think and feel of the customer experience and their experience as employees
   - Voice of Process (VOP): track, measure, and monitor what your processes say about the customer experience and the employee experience (e.g., number and reason of cancellations/returns, or speed of cases resolution, etc.)

In the O of Growth, we'll talk about how to operationalize these.

What you often find when starting this type of review is that what will make your customer's life happier and easier will also improve your processes, and that will eventually save costs or increase revenue.

The **KPN Next of Kin** project we saw in Chapter 12 shows precisely this dynamic.

Susan Oudshoorn, KPN CX Lead, shared with us:

> When we started the Next of Kin project, there was a growing awareness that if we wanted to build a relationship with our customers, we needed to make a significant impact on moments that matter for them: life-changing moments such as moving, getting married, expecting your first child, but also going into pension [or] dying. By really understanding the context of such an event, we were able to make a human connection and pleasantly surprise our customers.

> Creating a memorable positive emotion around such an event has a significant impact on how our customers and our employees perceive our company. We started the Next of Kin project because there was a lot to optimize in our processes around this event, such as our tone of voice, our empathy skills, and our data (storage). The latter to prevent very painful errors such as wishing a deceased person a happy birthday or asking him how he appreciated our service.

Before the Next of Kin project, KPN customers needed to place multiple calls to different numbers for each subscription that needed cancellation. Through this project, one central dedicated "*nabestaande desk*" was set-up to make that next-of-kin call much easier and more relational thanks to the new empathy skills.

2. Stay grounded during your growth by continuously keeping the focus on your strategy and actions, and by regularly reassessing your course and the elements above

UPIC Health built its success around tracking call dispositions (also called reason codes) and matching the Voice of Process with the Voice of Customers; this approach provided their clients with valuable customer insights never had before, and enabled them to both reduce costs and provide better patient care.

An incredibly underutilized source of insights in your organization is your contact center. Here are two simple tips from us on how to access data from this treasure chest:

- visit the center to listen to or even answer some customer calls questions. This action will have a positive impact on the connection center employees, and it will spark your creativity for innovations.
- study the data (and eventually use text and speech analytics) to track and analyze why customers are contacting you. (We are

astonished at how many contact or connection centers we have visited that still do not track and regularly review contact reason codes.)

GROUNDING CHECK-IN

We have designed the following short assessment to help you have a check-in moment to review your current *Yellow Factor* readiness and potential and establish a reasonable target and action plan.

You can also take the assessment online at www.wownow.eu/HappinessGrowthAssessment

"HAPPINESS GROWTH" ASSESSMENT ©

For each assessment statement assign a score 1 to 5 for your Actual (A) and Potential (P) based on the following question:

Thinking of the following statements, to what degree and how regularly do you observe the following activities occurring in your organization?

1 = Not at all/Not yet/Never   2 = Partly/At times

3 = Mostly/Usually   4 = Almost fully/always

5 = Completely & Always

WHY AWARENESS & ALIGNMENT	A	P
1.1 Different levels within our company (from management to contact center advisors) are aware of the importance and impact of happiness on both customers and employees		
1.2 Different levels within our company (from management to contact center advisors) are aware of the impact they can drive for customers, employees, and society, know how they can increase happiness in business and are committed to happiness driven growth		
1.3 All our company partners and suppliers are aware of the importance and impact of happiness on both our customers and employees; they are aware of the impact they can drive for our customers, employees, and society, know how they can increase happiness in business and are committed to happiness driven growth		

WHY? REMARKS & ACTIONS TO ACHIEVE YOUR POTENTIAL AND A MID-TERM TARGET

WHAT – ASSESS YOUR *YELLOW FACTOR* READINESS	A	P
2.1 We can increase happiness in business through **HEALTH,** know what we can do here, and we have *Yellow Goldfish* in this category		
2.2 We can increase happiness in business through **AUTONOMY**, know what we can do here, and we have *Yellow Goldfish* in this category		
2.3 We can increase happiness in business through **PURPOSE**, know what we can do here, and we have *Yellow Goldfish* in this category		
2.4 We can increase happiness in business through **PLAY**, know what we can do here, and we have *Yellow Goldfish* in this category		
2.5 We can increase happiness in business through **INTEGRITY**, know what we can do here, and we have *Yellow Goldfish* in this category		
2.6 We can increase happiness in business through **NATURE**, know what we can do here, and we have *Yellow Goldfish* in this category		
2.7 We can increase happiness in business through **EMPATHY**, know what we can do here, and we have *Yellow Goldfish* in this category		
2.8 We can increase happiness in business through **SIMPLICITY**, know what we can do here, and we have *Yellow Goldfish* in this category		
2.9 We can increase happiness in business through **SMILE**, know what we can do here, and we have *Yellow Goldfish* in this category		

WHY? REMARKS & ACTIONS TO ACHIEVE YOUR POTENTIAL AND A MID-TERM TARGET

HOW - AMPLIFY GROWTH	A	P
3.1 GROUNDING: We have a clear vision, mission, values, strategy, and action plan and we choose your employees and target customers in alignment with our Happiness Driven Growth Strategy		
3.2 REACHING-UP: We challenge existing paradigms and ways of doing things; we help our people see things from different perspectives; we adopt new ways of thinking and working, by using human-centered approaches and methodologies; we empower our people with happiness knowledge, skills, and frameworks		
3.3 OPERATIONALIZING: We develop and master the six competencies (1. Shared understanding, 2. Experience design, improvement & innovation, 3. Empowerment, 4. Enablement, 5. Measurement & ROI, 6. Culture) in a coordinated, consistent, and continuous way.		
3.4 WOW BLOSSOMING: We Wow our employees and customers with experiences that actually contribute to their Happiness; we connect authentically through empathy with colleagues and customers; we acknowledge and celebrate new behaviors		
3.5 TAKING TIME: We take time to learn, to research, to work as a team, to test, to validate, to ask and listen, to reflect, and adjust accordingly. And we take care of ourselves and ensure all our people take time to care for themselves.		
3.6 HARVESTING: We acknowledge and celebrate great results, share stories, measure impact and reward based on happiness contribution		

WHY? REMARKS & ACTIONS TO ACHIEVE YOUR POTENTIAL AND A MID-TERM TARGET

OPEN QUESTIONS
4.1 Which of the above activities is your current biggest priority (if any)? Why? What can you do to progress it?
4.2 Which of the above activities is your current biggest challenge (if any)? Why? What can you do to overcome it?

CHAPTER 17

REACHING-UP

"The most common source of mistakes in management decisions is the emphasis on finding the right answer rather than the right question."

Peter Drucker

Reaching up

Crescere

Just as flowers need to reach up to grow after germination, companies need to Reach-up and become empowered. You can lead and help your company do this by:

1. **Reframing**: Challenging existing paradigms and ways of doing things and helping your team see things from different perspectives.
2. **Adopting new ways of thinking, working, and leading:** Dismissing old standards that no longer serve you and using human-centered approaches and methodologies like Design Thinking instead; practicing the ability to move fluidly between being a Transactional and a Transformational Leader.[145]
3. **Empowering your team with knowledge, skills, and frameworks:** Using tools such as customer archetypes, customer needs pyramid and customer journeys.

As we have seen in Chapter 1 (The Evolution of Business) over the past few decades, companies have adopted different management approaches and philosophies about the center of their business: profits, customers, employees, and purpose. While there are still many people believing in and companies operating in the ways of Business 1.0 approach, there is a growing number of people and companies pursuing Happiness first (Business 5.0).

As more companies embrace the transformation and differentiate on Happiness, the more companies will need to transform to keep up. It's only a matter of time and relevancy, so the question is, "Will you lead or follow?"

---

145 You can read more about this practice in *Peak* by Chip Conley and about the two types of leader in *Leadership* by MacGregor Burns

In chapters 1 and 2, we aimed to provide you enough scientific and business background about the value of Happiness to raise awareness within your organization and to help understand the importance of such a transformation even for top management without a vision considering the emotional impact. The next step is for your company to start adopting approaches that support *Happiness Driven Growth*.

In this chapter, we want to briefly share essential new tools and methodologies that you can use. We will focus mainly on Design Thinking, Human-Centered Design, and the Double-Diamond process they both use. *Yellow Goldfish* such as the GE MRI Adventure scan for kids, Zaans Medical Centre, the New Sandy Hook Elementary School, and KPN's Next of Kin were made possible through a combination of Design Thinking and Human-Centered Design Approaches.

Later in Operationalizing, we will see how you can bring these tools into regular practice.

For now, let's look at a brief definition and one best practice example for each factor under Reaching-up.

1. REFRAMING

Reframing is seeing the current situation from a different perspective. It promotes innovation and creativity, and it can be tremendously helpful in problem-solving, decision making, and learning.[146] Reframing forces you to harness your creative and innovative thinking to achieve breakthrough solutions. It is original, out-of-the-bowl thinking!

Reframing also can help you move on more constructively from a situation where you may feel stuck or confused. It can be beneficial

---

146 More info on www.managementisajourney.com/reframing-for-innovative-and-creative-problem-solving/

for front-line employees to see things from different perspectives and be better able to empathize with the customer.

Reframing aims to shift one's perspective to be more empowered to act–and hopefully to learn at the same time.

REFRAMING ANGER DURING CONTACT CENTER TRAINING

Rosaria and Kathy van De Laar from EarlyBridge delivered an empathy training to Wolters Kluwer's outsourced contact center (Online Now) in Tirana, Albania. When they asked the employees to identify and respond to customers' emotions, they observed that there was a strong tendency to assume the main customer feeling was anger. "Oh, all our customers are just angry," the employees would say. And we cannot empathize with an emotion like anger.

Applying learnings from Rosenberg's NVC (Non-Violent Communication), Rosaria created a simplified framework. She distinguishes emotions in two broad categories: the ones we feel whenever our needs are met (happiness and love) and the ones we feel when our needs are not met (sadness and fear). See image. When customers are expressing sadness or fear, and instead of feeling acknowledged or understood, they feel judged, their emotions can escalate into anger.

By reframing anger and identifying instead which emotion is behind the anger, it becomes possible to empathize with the customer.

The training was started by asking each employee about their why and their background (also what is called seeding). Trainers learned that most of the employees had a University Degree in Law. This insight enabled the trainers to link the customer experience to the employee's own experience. They asked the employees to recall what they felt when preparing for their exams, how they valued every day, and to imagine what the customer – a lawyer needing a book to prepare for a bar exam only taking place once a year – may feel in case of delay. The comparison helped the employees genuinely get into the customer's shoes and feel real empathy for the customer. It connected them to the customer's **fear** increasing at any passing day and gave them an understanding of why they could perceive that as **anger** during the conversation. That, in turn, allowed the employee to consider a creative solution to address the customer's need behind that emotion.

Figure 6. Simplified Emotions Overview Based on Non-Violent Communication Methodology[147]
Source: Rosaria Cirillo, Wow Now

2. ADOPTING NEW WAYS OF THINKING, WORKING, AND LEADING

Design thinking is about a **methodology** about a **mindset** and a **changing paradigm** in management theory, moving from the traditional top-down and quantitative approach to a more bottom-up, qualitative approach in innovation and transformation processes.

---

147 www.wownow.eu/customer-understanding/

The basic idea of design thinking is that interdisciplinary teams can create outstanding innovations. It is a solution-focused method used to solve complex problems by profiting from different expert perspectives.

Jeffrey Tjendra says about the origins of design thinking:

> **Design thinking** is created because big corporations lack the ability to be creative and, in extreme cases, aren't able to create new products and services that meet the unmet needs of their customers. Because [of] how they are bred, a majority of corporations operate with **analytical thinking** where they are continually being disrupted by changing trends and consumer values rendering their business obsolete. Think of Kodak's film camera business. This happens because organizations lack value creation capability that would allow them to respond in time. To respond to external change is to innovate. To innovate, businesses must have the capacity to design. To design, they need to fuse design internally within the organization to create a culture that fosters creative thinking and actions with design methods and tools designers use.
>
> Pioneers like Tim Brown and Roger Martin have spearheaded the shifting role of design in business from noun to verb, where design can be used as a differentiator to respond to changing trends and consumer behaviors while gaining a competitive advantage that ultimately impacts bottom-line and drives business growth.[148]

For the **human-centered design approach,** the ultimate goal is to drive a customer focus deep within a corporation. The perspective of design thinking is broader than the one of human-centered design.

---

148 www.wired.com/insights/2014/04/origins-design-thinking/

The former focuses on innovation and creation and is about developing new products, services, and even solutions for social problems. The focus of the latter is on improving the usability and user experience of a specific product or service.[149]

Ultimately the two methodologies have much in common and can be combined. Whether you use Design Thinking or other methods, like Lean or Six Sigma, the core **Human-Centered Design Process** includes the following elements:

- A **problem-solving process that incorporates the needs** of customers, employees, and business stakeholders and demands the involvement of user and stakeholders in all stages of the development process—from analysis to evaluation
- A **way of working** that creates and refines real-world solutions
- A **Methodology** that follows a **predefined set of steps**
    1. **Research:** to understand the needs and motivations of
        - Customers
        - Employees and external partners (especially if the project requires changes to internal processes and behaviors)
    2. **Analysis:** to create artifacts (personas and customer journey maps) or other visual models to synthesize the research data
    3. **Ideation**: to generate ideas (though co-creation and crowdsourcing)

---

149 www.code-n.org/blog/design-thinking-human-centered-design-how-to-combine-benefits-both-approaches-product-innovation/

4. **Prototyping:** to prioritize the most feasible and impactful idea and consolidate it into a prototype to test on the target audience

5. **Reiterative Feedback:** to continuously gather feedback, adjusting prototype and retesting on the target audience until a final solution or pivoting

6. **Final product/service/experience**

Because of the alternation of Diverge and Converge in the steps from Discover to Define to Develop to Deliver, the Human-Centered Design Process is also called the "Double-diamond Design Process."[150] Here's how it goes—it

- **Starts** from a singular point (the initial focus of the project): problem definition.
- **Diverges,** as the research uncovers new insights and potential problems to solve.
- **Converges** in a middle point as teams synthesize the research findings and reframe the project focus.
- **Diverges** again as teams brainstorm a broad range of possible solutions and start to prototype.
- **Converges** again to its final point (the design solution) through multiple rounds of prototyping and testing.

150 www.slideshare.net/crrmic015/design-thinking-process-51674725

DESIGN THINKING AND A $25 INCUBATOR

This story is from a blog post by Patrick Sirois:[151]

> Students at the Stanford d. school were challenged to design a less expensive incubator for babies born prematurely in Nepal. The students traveled to Nepal to meet with families and doctors and see the problem for themselves. During the trip, they were exposed to the angst of parents who were not able to save their premature babies. This mission of empathy helped them define who the users were and what their problem was. The students discovered that there were, in fact, many donated incubators in the hospitals, but surprisingly they were mostly empty. They realized that less expensive incubators would not solve the problem since most premature babies were born far from hospitals, in rural areas, without access to incubators regardless of their cost.
>
> The students changed their perception of what was needed and began to think about how babies in rural areas could stay warm for long periods of time. They used pictures, videos, and storytelling of their experiences visiting Nepal to pinpoint the exact problem and brainstorm solutions. They stopped thinking of the doctors as their users and started thinking about desperate parents who need to give their babies a chance to survive. With each innovation or prototype that was suggested, they went back to the question on their whiteboard: *Are we helping parents in rural areas save their babies' lives?*
>
> The design that was eventually chosen was for an infant warmer that looks like a mini sleeping bag. It is made of a

151 www.blog.triode.ca/2015/01/21/design-thinking-and-a-25-incubator-a-case-study/

> material that holds in heat. It can be thrown into a pot of boiling water to get hot, and then it will retain the heat for a few hours. The baby is wrapped tightly inside the warmer, with a special hood to keep the face exposed [but still provide warmth for] the baby's head. This simple device keeps the baby warm during the time it takes for the parents to reach the nearest hospital, even if it's a few hours away.
>
> The students who undertook this project didn't stop with a prototype. They formed a company called Embrace and started manufacturing the product, which sells for a mere $25. **Embrace**[152] now has programs in eleven different countries and has helped over 50,000 premature and low birth weight infants.

It all started with the design thinking process, and the result is an easy-to-use medical device that has the potential to save millions of newborns in developing countries.[153]

DESIGN THINKING AND VALIDATION IN KPN'S NEXT OF KIN PROJECT

The KPN Next of Kin Project that we shared in the WHAT Chapter about Empathy used Design Thinking methodology and reiterative process.

A key element we want to highlight in the Design Thinking process is the importance of validating initial ideas through prototype and reiterative feedback, regularly checking back with customers to validate assumptions. KPN's Next of Kin Project shows an excellent example in practice.

---

152 www.embraceglobal.org/about-us/

153 www.slate.com/blogs/the_eye/2013/11/04/embrace_infant_warmer_creative_confidence_by_tom_and_david_kelley.html

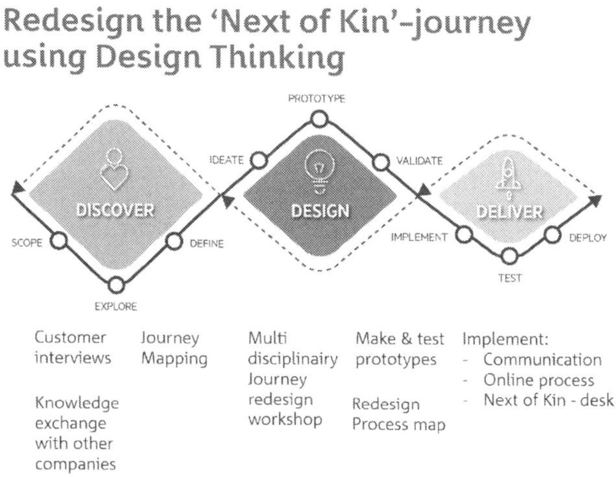

Figure 7. Source: KPN "Next of Kin" project led by Heike Faber (Lead Designer) and Susan Oudshoorn (Ex CX Lead) and Erik Vercouteren (Ex VP CX)

Susan Oudshoorn, KPN Ex CX Lead, shared with us:

> For this project, we applied the Design Thinking process. Before the project, customers wanting to cancel a subscription for a deceased would call the regular 'save' desk: a desk that tries to keep customers from churning once they have contacted KPN to end some (or all) of their services. This desk has no formal training in 'having an empathic conversation' on this level and was mostly concerned with people who were going to a competitor instead of people that just went through a major life event.
>
> Since different services have different notice periods, that made people uncertain whether other subscriptions would end too, which generated repeated calls.
>
> To end the subscription, customers needed to provide a "death certificate" by physical mail. Weeks could go by between the call and the arrival of the certificate. The certificate was mostly not accompanied by a letter that

matched it which a specific 'call' or customer. The cancellation came into effect from certificate arrival plus one-month notice. This process had a high error rate on the processing side and created a lot of repeat calls.

The explorative customer interviews gave us a rich context of the events and insight into the customer experience of the contact with KPN and other companies; we looked at what was perceived as 'basic,' what was annoying, what was really upsetting and what was warm and unexpected.

The 'death certificate' was one of the most surprising things for us. We expected people to find having to provide one a hassle. We expected people not to have enough copies, not be able to find the thing, etc. In the customer interviews, none of the customers actually complained about the certificate. When asked about it, they said they found it logical and even reassuring ('otherwise my angry ex-wife could report me as deceased and end my subscription'). And they were asked to send in the certificate by every company they approached after the event.

As it turned out, the points of complaint were that customers **needed to send the certificate by physical mail** and that each subscription had a different notice period, creating confusion on the timing of the cancellation. So, the process adjustments KPN made based on this new customer insights were:

- To allow customers to photograph the certificate and send it by email, even while they were still on the phone with the operator
- To send a KPN confirmation email right after the call, because, having to call about five or ten companies to

end various subscriptions, people didn't remember which company asked or said what

- To limit the contact notice period 'within five working days' from cancellation request, instead of 'one month from the 1st of the following month' and to apply the same notice period for all the products (mobile, internet and TV)

3. EMPOWERING

a. **Train all your employees** to understand the impact needs psychology, brain chemistry, and emotions have on experiences and how they each can contribute to the happiness (for the internal employee and the external customer).

b. **Train all your customer-facing employees to identify and respond to customer needs and emotions** using emotional intelligence. This skill can help them identify, assess, and control their own and their customer's emotions and enables them to respond with empathy and care to find a workable solution that addresses customer needs.

c. **Empower your team with knowledge, skills, and frameworks** like your customer archetypes, your customer needs pyramid, and customer journey maps to transform the way they can understand and support customers (and themselves too).

TREAT OTHERS LIKE THEY WANT TO BE TREATED: BRAND BIOLOGY

Brand Biology, a UK empathy training provider, has debunked the application of the Golden Rule "treat others like YOU would like to be treated" in contact centers. This approach only works if you are dealing with someone like you, and, when creating contact center scripts and rules, only if every customer would be the same. But they are not. We are not the same. We are individuals. And we are all different. Applying the Bradford and Bingley Personality Framework (which identifies four different archetypes), Brand Biology helps contact centers use the new approach of "Treat others like THEY want to be treated," or Platinum Rule. How can you know how others want to be treated? Here are three steps to determine your actions:

- identify their archetype: Is the person a Controller, a Feeler, a Thinker, or an Entertainer?
- understand what drives their archetypical reactions and behavior in any given circumstance
- act and react according to that type, while still being true to your characteristics

Brand Biology has proven that contact center agents can create more fulfilling interactions for both customer and employee, when they are able (thanks to training and applying this framework) to recognize the type of archetype they are speaking with and to react accordingly, while still staying true to the personal self. The reciprocal empathy and connection established are the enabling factor. Ultimately this process generates more revenue by creating excellent CX. Brand Biology was named Best Customer Experience Training Company at the 2017 UK Customer Experience Awards.[154]

154 www.cxm.co.uk/winner-focus-brand-biology/

CHAPTER 18

OPERATIONALIZING

"Happiness is a business model."

Tony Hsieh

Operationalizing

Rendere operativo

While **G**rounding and **R**eaching-up are about **knowing what to do**, **O**perationalizing is about **actually doing it** in a coordinated, consistent, and continuous way.

DEVELOPING AND MASTERING SIX HAPPINESS COMPETENCIES

Forrester research shows that if you deliver the right CX reliably time after time, you need to progress from rigorously having established six CX competencies to advancing and deepening them into the organization. That requires investing in best practices and executing with precise and intentional cadence, accountability, and coordination, focusing on what's most important for your customer's experience and your business's success.[155] The same is true for *Happiness Driven Growth©*. To move up the needs pyramid and achieve both customer and employee happiness, we have identified six Happiness competencies[156] companies need to master:

1. Understanding
2. Design
3. Empowerment
4. Enablement
5. Measurement
6. Culture

155 Source: Forrester Report Why and How to Lead a CX Transformation. The Executive Overview of the CX Transformation Playbook by David Truog, 2017

156 The model we present in this chapter is an adaptation of the six CX disciplines framework (Strategy, Customer Understanding, Experience Design, Measurement, Organizational Adoption, and Culture) initially established by Forrester and CXPA. This "Driven" model is covered in more details in the *Wow Now HCX Masterclass Compendium: Your concise guide to Human-Centered and Happiness-Contributing Experience Leadership,* available on Amazon (ASIN B08NTS9TX2)

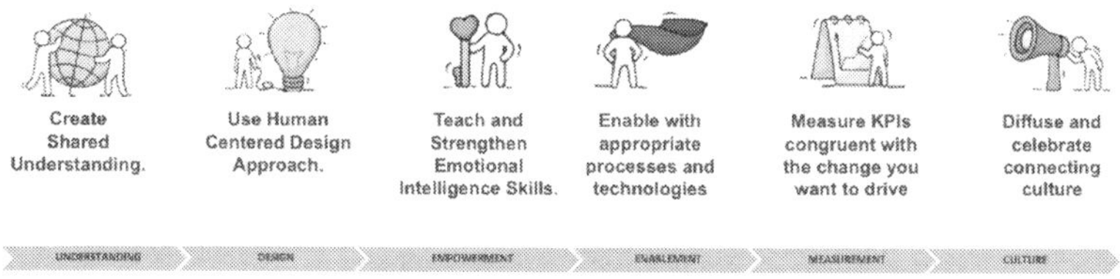

Figure 8. Source: Rosaria Cirillo, Wow Now

Let's look at each of these competencies one by one.

1. Understanding. Ensure everyone in the organization has the **same shared understanding** of who your customers and employees are, what they need and how they feel; about how they perceive the experience with your company, how you can serve them in a way they can appreciate, and if/how you can either improve the experience or help them reframe their perception of the experience; of your company mission, brand values, customer promises, and what's expected from everyone in the organization

You can create a shared understanding by:

- **Collecting** data and insights through VOC (Voice of Customer), VOE (Voice of Employee), and VOP (Voice of the Process), and through regularly, directly experiencing the experience your company is providing (so-called "immersions"),
- **Analyzing** both quantitative and qualitative data using different methodologies and turning them into actionable insights
- **Documenting** the insights in easily digestible formats (e.g., though Persona and Customer Journey Maps)
- **Sharing** within the organization, at all levels, among employees and partners).

To complement quantitative insights coming from NPS Surveys, **Aegon** gained significant insight into their customers' perception of the company by hosting Customer Arenas. They then created an incredibly emotional video using photos and quotes collected from their customers during these sessions and used that video to share the new insights within the organization. Aegon is an insurance company that could be perceived as—and of course, partly is—numbers and ratio driven. Yet, thanks to this video, everyone could feel, in a very visual, musical, and emotional way, that Aegon sees itself as a life-events company and is on a transformation journey to be emotions and value-driven. This video has been shared across the company, and it's included in onboarding training in some countries.

At **Airbnb,** each employee receives $500 a quarter to spend on Airbnb to make sure everyone directly experiences Airbnb from a customer point of view and "*drinks their own champagne.*"

At **KPN,** everyone in the CX team has a private phone subscription with the operator (which they then expense back to the company) to make sure that they experience their services as customers do.

2. **Design:** use a Human-Centered Design approach to design and innovate experiences. In Reaching-up (Chapter 16), we saw these approaches and methodologies from a knowledge perspective and shared two examples of how they were applied. This stage is about putting them into action: any time a new experience is introduced, or an existing experience is changed in a significant way, companies must follow a defined/formal customer experience design process and use tools like Persona, Storytelling, and Customer/Employee Journey Mapping.

3. **Empowerment:** Provide employees and partners with the knowledge, space, budget, freedom, and the authority they need to make the right decisions and take the appropriate action at any given moment to deliver the right experiences.

In Chapter 4, we saw the value of Southwest Airlines' *Yellow Factor*: funny flight safety announcements. These are possible because the company empowers its employees to create what Chip and Dan Heath call "Defining Moments," resulting in happy employees, loyal flyers, and higher revenues.

Southwest has empowered their frontline to act on the spur of the moment and deliver these unique experiences. There's a culture of spontaneity that's fostered and encouraged. What's important to know about cultivating these kinds of moments is that they also come from owning a sense of individuality while representing the company. When it comes to peak moments, some may even expect this kind of experience while flying Southwest, but it has to be a thoughtful moment that's not continuously replicated. This kind of thing can only happen when you trust your frontline and give them some "wiggle room" to allow them to put their stamp on an unexpected experience.[157]

Ladies and Gentlemen (employees) of **The Ritz-Carlton Hotels** are empowered to delight guests by attending to their expressed and unexpressed wishes and needs thanks to the $2,000 per guest per day budget any Lady or Gentleman has, as we have seen in Autonomy.[158]

4. **Enablement:** enable employees with resources and tools to respond as needed from both a process and a technology point of view. Be mindful that the experience you want to deliver is supported by the 3 Ps: policies, processes, and procedures. Here we want to focus on one of the P's often most overlooked when designing a positive experience: procedures. A procedure consists of the step-by-

---

157 www.customerbliss.com/create-power-moments-dan-heath/
158 Source: Alec Dalton, Global Quality Improvement Manager at Marriott

step tasks involved to complete a process. They are often set-up at the workflow level, and they usually make the difference between "easiness" and "effort" of an experience as well as impact activities costs.

At **Ritz-Carlton Hotels**, when problems arise, a final step is taken by Ladies and Gentlemen after ensuring the satisfaction of their guests. Employees are required to record the guest incident in a global customer relationship management database. This procedure serves three purposes, all tied to creating happy experiences for all guests. First, every hotel will review the profiles of incoming guests to see if they experienced problems in a past stay with Ritz-Carlton; the hotels then act to ensure the problem does not recur in future visits. Second, each hotel regularly reviews themes in guest incidents and conducts process improvement and quality management exercises to reduce such issues locally. Third, at the global level, corporate operations leaders perform similar activities to redefine policies, processes, and programming that can ensure guest experiences globally meet the needs of the guests.[159]

5. **Measurement**: Once you have designed and delivered the wished experience in alignment with your Understanding and Strategy, you need to consistently measure how effectively you are providing the experiences.

a) **ensure the Key Performance Indicators you set are congruent with the change you want to drive**, both externally and internally. Two practical examples of this are:

- have your customer surveys include perception metrics and space for qualitative input collection,

159 Source: Alec Dalton, Global Quality Improvement Manager at Marriott

- don't place undue emphasis on metrics like Average Handle Time at contact centers, nor prioritize only short-term bottom-line metrics as overall business measures.

In 1988, Bob Chapman, chairman, and CEO of Barry-Wehmiller Companies, author of *Everybody Matters*, began an initiative to develop a truly human organization. He decided that the most important metric for him to track in his organization was the reduction in the divorce rate among his employees.[160]

Barry-Wehmiller Companies guiding principle is, "*We measure success by the way we touch the lives of people.*" Chapman realized how critical the business plays in the lives of his people when he visited a plant and spoke to one of his people about what's changed since Barry-Wehmiller Companies had taken over.

"My wife is talking to me!" one employee explained and added: "I now realize that, before you bought this company, I felt not valued for 30 years. I was told what to do. No one ever asked me what I thought. If I gotten things right and one thing wrong, I got told off. Now when I'm asked and tell them what I think, they listen to me. I feel good about myself when I go home."

Chapman believes that "How we treat our people affect how they treat their family,"[161] and that is very much the essence of why we think we need to focus on happiness first.

b) **Define what and when you want to measure, and which combination of three types of metrics** to use. See the table below for definitions and examples of *descriptive*, *perception,* and *outcome* metrics to measure CX.[162] Equivalent metrics apply to measure your EX (Employee Experience).

---

160 www.cx-journey.com/2012/07/truly-human-leadership-everyone-matters.html

161 www.strategicdiscipline.positioningsystems.com/blog-0/management-to-leadership-bob-chapman-san-antonio-scaleup-summit

162 www.wownow.eu/metrics-measurement-roi/

3 types of metrics matrix

Metrics type	WHAT	Metrics used
Descriptive metrics	What really happened?	Call & email volume SL, AR, waiting time Average call time FTR (1st time resolution) or OCS (1 call solution) Website visits / Usage Average Pages x visit
Perception metrics	What customer thinks and feels about what happened?	**CSAT** (Customer Satisfaction) **CEXPI** (Customer Experience Index) **CES** Customer Effort score **UGC** (User goal completion) Other Value or Contribution metrics
Outcome metrics	What customers are going to do as a result of their experience?	**PREDICTIONS**: - **NPS** (recommend) - Likelihood to repurchase/switch **ACTUALS**: - Churn (Renewal) rate/ Cancellations - Upsell/Upgrade - Referrals

Source: Wow Now 2015, elaboration of Forrester 3 types of Customer Experience Metrics, in Outside-in from H. Manning & K. Bodine

Figure 9. Source: Rosaria Cirillo, Wow Now

c) **Consider new measures** which are more focused on Happiness.

In *Happier*, Tal Ben-Shahar explains: "Money and fame are subordinate and secondary goals to happiness. There would be no reason to seek them if they did not contribute, in some way, toward happiness." Whether our desires are material or social, they are merely a means toward an end: happiness. He continues, "Through evaluating how happy something makes us, we have a common currency that enables us to compare seeming unrelated experiences."

How do we know if we are operating at the top of the pyramid, maximizing everyone's happiness and business growth? We need to *measure what matters*!

Joseph Stiglitz said, "*What we measure informs what we do. And if we measure the wrong thing, we are going to do the wrong thing.*" Companies are using metrics that are no longer enough. They don't focus on the top of the pyramid. And they overemphasize the importance of "score."

Institutions and governments have started setting up various Happiness indexes, which are often complex. Within companies, we need to keep it simple, actionable, and relevant. We need to make visible (if and) how much we are contributing to happiness.

Wouldn't it be great if we were to be able to measure how much each company's interaction contributes to their customers and their employees' happiness?

Wouldn't it be a more meaningful "score" objective if we could say to our employees "let's improve our Happiness Contribution™" and know that when we increase it, customer purchases and ultimately business growth and profit will increase too?

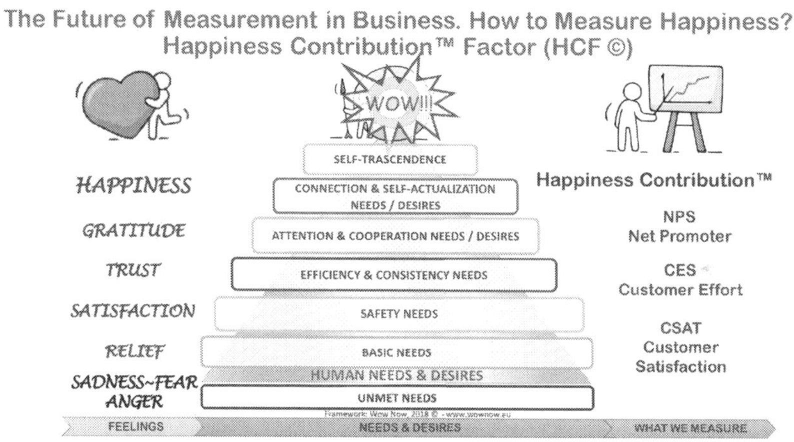

Figure 10. Source: Rosaria Cirillo, Wow Now

That is why in 2016 Rosaria defined a new metric - *Happiness Contribution™ Factor (HCF)*. The metric focuses on the emotional impact of the interaction on both the customer and the employee. It aims precisely at measuring whether interactions, experiences and relationships with companies (but also with schools, municipalities, city halls, countries) contribute to the happiness of both customers and employees. As mentioned in her TEDx talk in May 2016, she wishes that by 2021 companies, organizations, universities, municipalities, and even countries will compete for the yearly "*Highest Happiness Contribution Award.*"[163]

6. **Culture:** create and maintain a system of shared values and behaviors that focus employees on contributing to happiness (internally and externally). Be clear on your company values and expected behaviors; lead the way through management involvement; be consistent on the way you celebrate and reward the behaviors you want to foster.

Rien Brus, Global VP of Customer Strategy at **Aegon**, has the best tip on how to handle "resistance" questions when introducing new behaviors. When he first introduced the "Customer License" system[164], Rien was asked by his colleagues whether the new program was mandatory or voluntary. His response? "It's not mandatory nor voluntary; it's just the way we do things around here." That is the essence of culture.

When Rosaria delivered the empathy training we mentioned earlier, both **Online Now**'s owner and **Wolters Kluwer**'s Head of Customer Operations with four members of his customer service management team joined the session, flying in from Milan and Rome to Tirana[165]. Being present allowed them to acquire additional communication skills and tools, to see the agent reactions as they learned about the impact of the new way of handling calls, and to coordinate with the local team the changes started by this training. The contact center employees had a natural initial push-back, as is bound to happen when delivering training that implies some changes in the status quo. When they started to say, "Oh, we can't do that because it will make the call take much longer" or "that's not what our procedure says,"

---

163 www.wownow.eu/tedxtalk-happiness-driven-growth/
164 As explained in Chapter 16 Grounding, this program requires every employee to spend two and half days every two years spending time with or talking directly to customers
165 Online Now is the outsourced contact center operating on behalf of Wolters Kluwer

the management team was there to step in. Giovanni Portaluri, Head of Wolters Kluwer Customer Operations, first acknowledged the employee's feelings and worries and then said: "We are committed to providing better remarkable customer experiences. We fully support changes coming with this training. If call handling minutes go up at the beginning, that's fine; if our procedures don't [properly] support or enable…such customer focus, let's look at which of them doesn't and see how we can change them." [166]

Nothing is more powerful than that to show the commitment to change and get the change started.

Celebration, like the Global Aegon Awards, explained in chapters Smile and Wow Blossoming, is also a great way to foster culture.

To master the six competencies and keep them alive in your organization, it's essential to:

- Activate and engage the team with fun experiential training to crystalize their learning.
- Find engaging ways to embed new practices in their daily routines and continuous workflow.

Rosaria addresses in more detail and practice each of these competencies in her recently published *Wow Now HCX Masterclass Compendium: Your concise guide to Human-Centered and Happiness-Contributing Experience Leadership,* available on Amazon.

Now let's look at some ways you can do so in the next chapter **Wow** Blossoming.

---

166 More details on this example on https://wownow.eu/exceptional-customer-service-leadership-example/

CHAPTER 19

WOW BLOSSOMING

"We are what we repeatedly do. Excellence, then, is not an act, but a habit."

Aristotle

Wow Blossoming
Fiorire

Wow Blossoming is about:

1. **Wowing** your employees and customers with experiences that actually contribute to their Happiness
2. **Connecting authentically through empathy** with colleagues and customers: doing the work and delivering experiences, **flourishing** as human beings thanks to the new knowledge, empowerment, and enablement
3. **Acknowledging** and celebrating new behaviors

1. & 2. WOWING AND FLOURISHING

In the nine chapters sharing WHAT, we saw many examples of Wowing employees and customers. In chapter 12, Empathy, we explored Empathy and Connection as one of the elements that contribute to our happiness. Empathy and Connection are also the core of the HOW when it comes to Wow Blossoming. In her book *Shame Resilience and the Power of Empathy*, Brené Brown defines Empathy as:

"The skill or ability to tap into our own experiences in order to connect with an experience someone is relating to us."

She also reports a definition by writers Arn Ivey, Paul Pederson, and Mary Ivey:

"The ability to perceive a situation from the other person's perspective. To see, hear, and feel the unique world of the other."[167]

Empathy is the ability to recognize and understand the feelings of others. It is the ability to feel what someone else is feeling—not only

167 Shame Resilience and the Power of Empathy, Brené Brown

to feel *for* someone but to feel *with* someone. In other words, it's walking in someone else's shoes.

Being vulnerable and having empathy serve to bring us closer and to connect with each other. And to be better leaders.

In her book *I thought it was just me (but it isn't)*, Brené Brown shares: "in the growing body of empathy research, we are finding that successful leaders often demonstrate high levels of empathy; empathy is related to academic and professional success; it can reduce aggression and prejudice and increase altruism; empathy is essential for building a meaningful, trusting relationship, which is something we all want and need."

Empathy is a skill we can all develop and practice to achieve connection with others and reinforce our sense of and need for belonging.

Brown defines ***Connection*** as:

"The energy that exists between people when they feel seen, heard, and valued; when they can give and receive without judgment; and when they derive sustenance and strength from the relationship."[168]

In her book *The Gifts of Imperfection*, Brown explains: "we are wired for connection. It's in our biology. From the time we are born, we need connection to thrive emotionally, physically, spiritually, and intellectually."

And this has been validated by the latest findings of neuroscience, as we have seen in Chapter 12.

Now let's see a few examples of this blossoming in practice.

---

168 *The Gifts of Imperfection*, Brené Brown

RITZ CARLTON AND JAKARTAN COOKIES

Alec Dalton, Global Quality Improvement Manager at Marriott, shared with us the following example of connection between a front-desk agent and a hotel guest.

A guest of The Ritz-Carlton Jakarta, Pacific Place, shared with a front desk agent his passion for sculpture and experiencing local cuisine throughout his travels. In the middle of his stay, the guest was surprised when presented with a handmade sculpture from a local marketplace; he was even further delighted by the accompanying plate of Jakartan cookies the front desk agent delivered to him. In a post-stay survey, the guest remarked about the warmth he felt from that very personal experience and about his affection for The Ritz-Carlton brand for recognizing his passions.

KPN NEXT OF KIN CALLS.

Susan Oudshoorn, KPN CX Lead, shared with us two examples of typical calls and interactions their dedicated team has:

1. One colleague, Erica, received a call from a man who had recently lost his wife. He, his late wife, and their 11-year-old son had moved back to the Netherlands for treatment for his wife. Since they weren't residents and the man had not worked in the country, he did not qualify for government aid. The man had no income, and therefore, he and his son would be evicted. Erica told the man about the "Widows and Orphans" support that they would qualify for (offered by a social insurance bank). Weeks later, this man called back to the desk to thank Erica and to tell that because of the support, they were able to stay in the Netherlands, his son could finish school here, and they

were able to keep visiting the resting place of their deceased family member.

Erica is sadly an experiential expert herself, having lost her husband and being a mother of two children. Being able to provide a listening ear to people who need it and especially being able to help people as she did with the father and son, is the reason why she, and she points out, many of her colleagues too, do this line of work. **It is meaningful and fulfilling to have a real impact on someone's life**.

2. Another colleague, Mellien, had a conversation with a man who called to end the TV subscription for his deceased mother-in-law. Mellien replied that they were able to terminate the subscription within a week. The son-in-law quickly replied that that was unwanted; he preferred to close the subscription one week later. That Sunday, a football match between two big clubs in the Netherlands would air. His mother-in-law and their family were supporters of one of the teams, while he supported the other team. He shared that they used to watch these matches together, and since the mother-in-law laid out in her living room, they could watch this important match together for a one-last-time experience! Mellien was able to accommodate his request.

Mellien feels it is significant that people share such personal stories. Even though they can be sad, they genuinely touch her, and in this instance, the story came with humor as well. **Mellien chose to work for the Next of Kin desk because of its more personal and human focus. This case reflects that for her**.

MONTREAL COMICCON ADHD ACCOMMODATIONS

Montreal ComicCon was launched in 2008. This fast-growing event, dedicated to pop culture, attracted over 60,000 visitors in 2017. It takes the form of a fan convention with multi-genre content focused on comic books, sci-fi, horror, manga/anime, toys, movies, video games, and the broad pop culture and entertainment worlds. The event attracts people of all ages who share the same interest: the pop culture world and all that it embraces.

Fans have the opportunity to come to meet their favorite creators from the world of comics, get their autographs, buy a sketch, or thank them for their work. Additionally, in one of the biggest draws, fans get to meet the personalities behind their favorite TV shows and movies. Celebrities participate in autograph and photo opportunities and Q&As in sessions that accommodate between 700 and 2,500 fans.

Their Accessibility policy provides accommodation that promotes independence and self-efficacy. Zipora Sarah Richman, one of their visitors, shared this story with us:

> I have severe ADHD and navigating the maze of a large event such as a ComicCon can be very stressful just because of the event itself. Large crowds, lots of stimulation, confusing directions, and the whole thing can be hard to navigate for the best of people. Not only were the staff themselves patient and helpful in creating a less stressful experience for me, but they also went above and beyond, ensuring I availed myself of all helpful accommodation they could provide. I walked up to disability services and said, "Hello, I have severe ADHD..." Before I could even finish speaking, the employee responded with, "This kind of event must be challenging for you, let me get you a badge that can help you bypass some of that."

> The problem that people with ADHD often run into is that they have issues with the same things that everyone struggles with, and so the expectation is that they choose not to work as hard to achieve the same level of success. Because the accommodation they need is one that would make everyone's life easier, there is a stigma attached to ADHD and accommodation. It was the first time in my life that I didn't have to explain why a stressful situation shouldn't be stressful for me. Not having to justify why it was so difficult made me feel more accepted than I can [ever before] remember feeling. The experience with this company also left me feeling as if I was a valued customer just by virtue of my patronage. I felt like they wanted me there, and they weren't obligated to do that. It's hard to explain but—more than anything else—**it was the way they fulfilled the need for the accommodation and the way they provided support: it was just implicitly understood and natural**.

"The way" Zipora refers to is what *Empathy* is all about and what Montreal ComicCon did for her—and other people with ADHD or other disabilities—is a beautiful example of *Yellow Factor*.

3. ACKNOWLEDGING AND CELEBRATING NEW BEHAVIORS

To gain momentum and keep morale high, spotlight small successes as employees display new habits, and feel proud when using the new skills. Share highlights and reward the behaviors you want to promote. Find ways to involve management to listen to calls regularly and even make or take calls themselves.

UPIC HEALTH PATIENT CARE

Juli Briskman, Chief Marketing Officer of UPIC Health, shared with us two examples of typical calls and interactions their team receives. These two calls have also been shared internally as examples of the exemplary empathetic behaviors they want to promote to help those in distress:

> #1: We recently had a call from a rape victim, and the response by our patient care team was excellent. The team member who picked up the call was a relatively new employee, and he helped the patient communicate through her grief, set up an appointment quickly, and reiterated several times that nobody should have to go through such trauma. We shared a recording of the call throughout the organization as an example of empathy for the patient. Our patient care team receives calls like this regularly: the team is equipped to handle them professionally, thanks to the organization's emphasis on empathy and non-judgment, through our speaker series, *UPICares work*, and regular training.

> #2: We also recently had a call from a young man who was very upset as he was told by a lover that he was exposed to HIV during their relations. Our patient care coordinator was able to direct him for immediate testing and strongly encouraged him to take immediate action and follow up with counseling. She also helped him complete patient registration over the phone, suggesting that it may be less stressful than face-to-face at the affiliate office. And she went a step further, showing an extreme capacity for empathy: "Your life is valuable," she said. "No one determines your self-worth but yourself. Let's make sure you are protected. As long as you are protected, there's

> nothing anyone can do to you." They were both crying by the end of the call.

GLOBAL AEGON AWARDS (GAA)

When new behaviors and projects are celebrated and shared, then learning grows and spreads to do better, just like casting seeds on fertile ground. When there are acknowledgment and reward for adopting the new behaviors or knowledge, the growth circle grows ever wider with exponential potential.

Aegon harnesses the power of sharing and learning from each other with initiatives like the GAA, which we explored in chapter 14. They also formally recognized such initiatives with the *One Aegon Award.* Rien Brus, Global VP Customer Strategy, explains:

> This new award is given to the country unit that has made the best use of learnings from other units. The reason we came up with the One Aegon Award was to give credit to the country or business unit that copies, pastes, begs, or borrows from other country units. We need more of it. I hope this award will encourage a lot more 'smart copying and pasting' in the future.

In the words of Aegon CEO Alex Wynaendts: "The year's awards ceremony may be over, the eight category winners may be now known, but the lessons learned, and ideas sparked, may be too numerous to count."

Now let's look at a critical enabler of growth in the next chapter **T**aking Time.

CHAPTER 20

TAKING TIME

"Life is too short to be in a hurry."

- Henry David Thoreau

Taking Time

Dedicare Tempo

There is a straightforward truth: driving change takes time. It takes time for the change to take place and for growth to happen, but it takes even more time to understand what the change needs to be and how it should look.

You need to take:

- time to define your seed and get grounded (Chapter 16),
- time to reframe and apply new methodologies (Chapter 17)
- time to Operationalize new ways of doing (Chapter 18)

so that you can Wow and Blossom (Chapter 19).

During all these stages, you need to take time to learn, to research, to work as a team, to test, to validate, to ask and listen, to reflect, and adjust accordingly. And you need to take care of yourself, as we saw in Health.

In his TEDx Talk, "Want to be happy? Be grateful", David Steindl-Rast poses questions around how to find a method to live gratefully, not just once in a while being grateful, but being grateful moment by moment throughout your entire life. He points out the simplicity of the method we were taught as kids to teach to our kids today about crossing a street: "Stop, look, go." He says that the main problem, the reason why we miss the opportunity to be grateful and happy, is that we don't stop! "We have to stop, we have to be quiet, and we have to build stop signs in our lives."

We have seen under **Health** (Chapter 6) the importance of sleep and under **Smile** (Chapter 14) the importance of taking time to acknowledge and award contribution and innovation.

These can only happen if we consciously allocate structural time and energy to them.

Across the examples that we have collected, we have identified at least six structural ways of *taking time* that are important to drive change and make a difference to our happiness and to contributing to the happiness of others.

Let's look at them one by one.

1. TAKING TIME-IN TO REFLECT

Have regular reflection moments about where you are and where you want to go. Time-in provides you with an opportunity, a reminder, to stop for a few minutes, to reflect on what you have experienced, and to look inside yourself.

In her book *The Gifts of Imperfection,* Brené Brown introduces an outstanding Gratitude Practice: TGIF (Trusting, Grateful, Inspires, Faith). She writes, and invites us to do the same, a weekly note about "what I'm trusting, what I'm grateful for, what inspires me, and how I'm practicing my faith." This practice can be applied in our business, too, as a way of reframing our regular TGIF.

2. TAKING TIME-OUT TO LEARN AND CONFRONT

Regroup with your team. Whenever possible, choose an inspiring location like a unique off-site location to look at the blossoming together, acknowledging everyone's contribution, and talking about what is needed to help turn the blossoms into ripe fruit that can be harvested. Take time out of your daily routine to KEEP LEARNING: attend courses, training, conferences, and do exchange visits in other companies.

3. TAKING TIME-ON TO DO AND OBSERVE

Spend time doing what you are most passionate about. Google allows employees to spend 20 percent of their time on projects they are passionate about.

Observe (and enjoy) your own blossoming: what did you do that got you here? What are you most proud of? What is working very well? What needs adjustment? What is different from what you expected and why? How can you adjust?

4. TAKING TIME-OFF TO ENJOY

The best time to take some time off and recharge your batteries is after enjoying blossoming and reflecting on what came from it.

In the WHAT chapters Health and Smile, we have seen examples of this with Qualtrics.

5. TAKING DOWNTIME TO RECHARGE REGULARLY AND LET CREATIVITY HAPPEN

In his HSA (Happiness Studies Academy) course, Tal Ben-Shahar shares about how important it is to take time for our well-being and our creativity, and how we can simply recharge—and need to do so—for short but repeated times during the day.

He emphasizes the importance of regular physical exercise, pointing out that workouts—as few as three weekly sessions of 30 minutes each—have the same effect as the most powerful psychiatric medication. If employees start a physical exercise regime, the workplace will be a happier, more creative, and less stressful place.

He also encourages employees to take regular breaks during the day. Being "on" all the time is not helpful for the individual employee, nor the organization. We need to recharge our psychological batteries. Creativity and productivity go down when there is no time for recovery throughout the day (15 minutes of downtime every hour or two), the week (at least one day off), and the year (a real vacation once every six or 12 months).

6. TAKING TIME UP TO CELEBRATE

And, of course, don't forget to celebrate and acknowledge all the changes you have made and also small successes you have achieved. Too often, we just move on from one project and one deadline to the other, without taking time to celebrate having completed the project or having met the deadline.

We have seen ways of celebrating in the WHAT Chapter Smile, and now in the HOW Chapter Harvest, we will share more details about how AEGON celebrates.

Let's see two examples of how Taking Time has made the difference in the examples we shared in WHAT.

THE TRIGGER FOR *GE* MRI SCAN

One of our favorite stories of "Taking Time ON" is the story told by Doug Dietz, the designer at GE Healthcare behind the GE-Adventure Series we saw in the Nature Chapter. A few years ago, he wrapped up a project working on a brand new, beautiful MRI machine, and while he was proudly waiting to see his design live in the hospital, he encountered a young patient in the hallway heading toward the scan room with her parents. She was clearly terrified, tears rolling down her face. Doug suddenly saw the situation through the eyes of the girl.

"The room itself is kind of dark and has those flickering fluorescent lights," he remembers in his TEDx talk. He added, "the machine that I had designed basically looked like a brick with a hole in it."[169]

This moment altered his perspective forever, and he knew he had to make a change. He enrolled in an executive education course at Stanford's d.school and learned how to approach the challenge from

169 See the TEDx on www.youtu.be/jajduxPD6H4

a human-centered design perspective that would ultimately help him make MRIs less terrifying for children.

A new challenge was born. How could Doug and his team create a scanner experience that children would love? From this new approach came a fantastic series of story adventures and decorated rooms that appeal to the five senses that await children needing an MRI. The child enters something like a pirate ship or canoe for the scan, their imaginations fired with an adventure story, and the scan is done with no stress, no trauma because Doug Dietz used human-centered design.[170]

Doug writes in his comment to his TEDx Talk, "The Adventure Series project at GE Healthcare has definitely been a blessing. We are nearing 100 installations, and most facilities have multiple rooms! I still love to work with the families and kids to develop the adventures. Immersing in the 'Empathy' of your users gives you the knowledge, passion, and heart to...I guess it brings tears to your eyes!"

Sometimes we don't realize that **what we create or develop has the potential to affect others' lives.**

The GE-Adventure Series wouldn't exist if Doug did not take the time to leave the office and go to the hospital to see his new "brick" MRI machine creation in the field and open his mind to a whole new perspective.

HOW AEGON TAKES TIME-OUT

Rien Brus, VP of Customer Strategy, has been relentlessly searching, learning, listening, testing, piloting, seeding within the organization and outside, for different ways in which he could transform the

---

170 www.thisisdesignthinking.net/2014/12/changing-experiences-through-empathy-ge-healthcares-adventure-series/ and www.challenges.openideo.com/challenge/creative-confidence/inspiration/the-story-of-doug-dietz-creative-confidence-in-the-mri-suite

company culture and approach to Customer Experience. He even went to Disney World to fully understand the Disney Magic and get inspiration about how he could bring that magic into the insurance and pension world.

By doing so, he has collected plenty of best practices. Here are a few:

- using Customer Arenas to gain better insight on customers voice and to have employee's direct involvement
- making an emotional video with customers' quotes and images to spread new insights within the company
- creating the "Customer License" program where back-office Aegon employees need to spend at least two and a half days every two years doing activities that require direct contact with customers
- creating the Manager Challenge where executives call two or three customers per month – generally, detractors who replied to the Net Promoter Score survey
- establishing the Customer Strategy Campus.

This extract from Aegon company magazine "Share" Spring 2017[171] shows how Aegon has been harnessing the power of taking extra time with each other in cross-country and cross-functional off-sites: *To achieve our strategic goals faster, we can and should make better use of each other's knowledge, experience, products, and services.*

Rien Brus says:

> As Global Vice President Customer Strategy, I am lucky to meet colleagues around the world. Often when I am in an Aegon country, I start by showing a slide of two apples. They are the same shape, the same size. In fact, they are

171 www.careers.aegon.com/contentassets/1e41abddf9cb427690ce751b6968db99/share20spring202017.pdf

> pretty much identical except that one is green and the other one is red. I ask: what is the first thing you notice? Nine out of ten times, the answer relates to the different colors.
>
> We tend to look for differences, rather than seeing the similarities. I believe that is what makes initiatives like the Customer Strategy Campus so important. We started the annual Customer Loyalty Forum in 2010. The seventh edition, held last October in The Hague, was extended from two days to three and given a new name. The changes reflect the broader range of topics covered and a more diverse group of participants in customer contact, experience, and insight roles. But most importantly, instead of merely listening to each other's best practices, as we had done in the past, the extra day allowed us to work together towards common solutions to real Aegon business challenges – a good example of all four Future Fit behaviors. These challenges ranged from hiring and retaining the ideal service center representative to making Future Fit actionable for colleagues who do not have contact with customers.

Most of Rien Brus' initiatives perfectly embody what we see as the critical seeds of *Happiness Driven Growth.* As he brought most initiatives to the Blossoming phase, he has also Taken the Time to Celebrate Success by acknowledging and rewarding the local initiatives that have spread within the organization.

To conclude, let's look at some of the results Aegon, and other companies we mentioned, have achieved, in the next chapter **H**arvesting, the final stage of Growth.

CHAPTER 21

HARVESTING

"And on the seventh day God had finished the work He had been doing; so on that day, He rested from all His work.... Then God blessed the seventh day and sanctified it, because on that day He rested from all the work of creation that He had accomplished...."

- Genesis 2:2-3

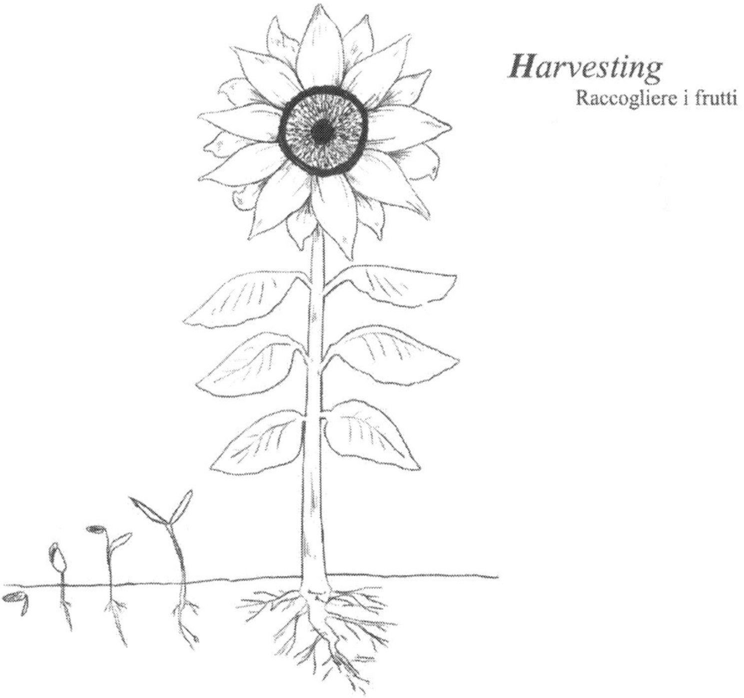

Finally, the last stage of growth is **H**arvesting your results and giving back.

Harvesting is really about seeing the *results*, celebrating them, and keeping the circle of growth expanding within your organization and outside, by giving back sharing your seeds.

Celebrate and share early results and take the time to assess and review to ensure this doesn't stay a one-off exercise but truly becomes a new way of gardening for your company on its transformation to Happiness Driven Growth.

In this chapter, we want to share with you:

1. the results and employee and customer quotes from the examples shared in WHAT and HOW.
2. examples of how trailblazer companies are giving back

1. SEEING AND CELEBRATING RESULTS

IMPACT OF GE MRI SCAN

Doug Dietz' Adventure Series – that we have seen in the WHAT (Nature Chapter 11) and in the HOW (Taking Time Chapter 20) sections – showed the incredible positive impacts both on patient happiness and on hospital efficiency. Patient satisfaction scores went up to 90 percent. Children do not suffer anxiety anymore during their MRI scans. Some of them even ask their parents if they can "come back tomorrow." The better designed experience makes it easier for children to hold still during the procedure, and that means less need to repeat a scan. Less anxiety means less demand for anesthesia, which is better for the children, and means more patients can be scanned each day, heavily impacting the financial side of the equation.

The experience of joy and playfulness before and during the scan also reduced the fear felt by the parents, who were anxious for their child. As Doug Dietz puts it: “If you got the child, you got the parent, and if you got the parent, you can get the child.” He now trains other GE employees to use design thinking and innovation methods in their teams.[172]

GLOBAL AEGON AWARDS (GAA)

The Awards in numbers:

- 2018 Numbers: almost 100 nominees,[173] 24 finalists from 18 countries/Business Units.
- 2016-2018 Numbers: close to 300 nominees, 83 finalists from 21 countries/ Business Units.
- 8 Awards:
    1. Best employee in customer service
    2. Best community engagement
    3. Best empowerment initiative
    4. Best improvement
    5. Best employee in support and staff
    6. Best innovation
    7. Most customer-centric team
    8. One Aegon Award

Across all nominations and finalists for 2018, Marjolein Droog, Senior Associate Customer Strategy at Aegon, and one of the CXPA

---

172 Source: www.thisisdesignthinking.net/2014/12/changing-experiences-through-empathy-ge-healthcares-adventure-series/
173 Nominees (or nominations) are the local finalists who submitted to win a global award. Locally we recognize many more people, teams, and projects! For example, the local awards in the Netherlands alone had 90+ applications in 2018

NL chapter co-founders, selected three finalists for us that show incredibly well how organizations can contribute to the happiness of employees, society, and customers.

Aegon Speak Up! – Aegon, Romania – finalist in the category *Best empowerment initiative*

The Romanian Aegon team found a way to build a more robust internal community by engaging employees in Aegon Speak Up! At these meetings, colleagues have a chance to interact and share stories beyond day-to-day matters after working hours. The benefits go beyond simply building a community. The speakers have an opportunity to create impact, develop their presenting skills, and after every session, participants donate a symbolic amount of money, which at the end of the year is donated to a chosen charity.

Cities and Longevity Platform – Mongeral Aegon, Brazil – winner of the category *Best community engagement*

Mongeral Aegon[174], our joint venture in Brazil, launched the Cities and Longevity platform to highlight the fact that while the older population is growing, cities are not prepared for the changing demographics. Showcasing the experience of the elderly, identifying good practices by municipalities, and training public managers are just some of the elements of the Cities and Longevity platform that will ensure that Brazilians are better prepared for the decades to come.

Panic Now! – Aegon Life, India – the winner of the category Most customer-centric team.

This customer service team in Aegon Life in India found a new way of reducing complaints and repeat calls to the call center, leading to

174 https://institutomongeralaegon.org/

greater customer happiness. They shifted from being reactive to being proactive by "panicking in time." This approach allows them to identify potential threats to customer satisfaction before they even arise, fixing problems at the root, and rewarding employees who successfully manage to pinpoint these threats.

All these initiatives truly contribute to increasing happiness within the world, with a butterfly effect extending beyond the person they interact with directly.

What can show this better than the direct quotes from some of the finalists right after the Global Aegon Awards ceremony? Here are four of them for you.

- "The experience at the GAA has been wonderful [...] for having the opportunity to travel to the Netherlands, getting to know Aegon, and taking part in the celebration. The host team at the GAA has been very welcoming and has done a great job!"
- "Great experience. It motivates me to set and achieve objectives that could lead to another nomination and participation next year."
- "We know that Aegon is a worldwide company. But there is nothing like feeling it as a participant of the GAA. Getting to know the colleagues from China, India, and so many other countries has been unique."
- "I am proud to be part of Aegon because of its value all around the world. The GAA was really awesome and motivating."

KPN NEXT OF KIN RESULTS

KPN can't quantify if the new desk has generated a reduction of cancellations because before setting up this desk, KPN did not flag these calls as next-of-kin calls. Routinely, they didn't know the reason for the cancellation (or didn't register it anywhere if they happened to know). They do, however, have some quantitative and qualitative evidence that this is working:

- **Quantitative**: FCR (first contact resolution): During the first week of 2018, 98 percent of the next-of-kin calls were handled within 24 hours with no-repeat calls. The save desk handling subscription cancellations experienced an 89 percent resolution during that same period. There also was a reduction in the number of calls and activities needed as the process got centralized to one team, and photos of the death certificate were able to be sent via email.
- **Qualitative**: The KPN CEO used to receive letters of complaint quite regularly from next of kin and widows/widowers receiving congratulations on their late spouse's birthday or who kept receiving mail in their late spouse's name. You can imagine the hurt and frustration levels these people experienced for them to sit down and write a letter to the CEO after several attempts to get their information corrected. Those letters are sporadic now.

UPIC HEALTH PATIENT CARE

Juli Briskman, Chief Marketing Officer of UPIC Health, shared with us some quotes from UPIC customers who appreciated the empathy they felt during their calls during challenging moments of their lives:

- "I called asking for a next day appointment, and when the lovely woman I spoke to found that no appointments were available, she took it upon herself to find me a same-day appointment [elsewhere]. I really appreciated the effort and initiative to get me as convenient and practical an appointment as possible."
- "I was blown away by the level of compassion and professionalism I received from every single person I was in contact with, from the first phone call to my actual visit. Planned

Parenthood is an invaluable service that I will continue to support and be grateful for."

- "All of the people I spoke to were very helpful in getting my appointment scheduled. I was also very nervous, and the person I spoke to helped to calm me down."

2. GIVING BACK

In nature, nearly every plant and flower produce seeds that continue the growth cycle.

It is or should be the same in business. Here is a shortlist of the best examples of giving back that we have observed in our research:

- **Qualtrics #5ForTheFight:** Qualtrics is inviting everyone everywhere to give $5 to fight against cancer. Write the name of the person you donate for on your hand and share the image on social media with #5ForTheFight. One hundred percent of every dollar donated goes directly to supporting groundbreaking cancer research, like the work of Dr. Joshua Schiffman. He is studying the fact that elephants don't get cancer to find out what that means for humans.[175] In the words of Qualtrics co-founder Ryan Smith:

  > We created a foundation called 5 For The Fight. What if ten million people gave five dollars? Or five euros. The Utah Jazz sent out a jersey with Qualtrics on it, and we were about ready to sign something, and someone on my team said, 'Hey, if we're really serious about cancer, why don't we put 5 For The Fight on the jersey?'
  >
  > I had to think about it for a second. We pay millions of dollars for that. And I do want my logo everywhere. But

175 www.5forthefight.org/

that was the point where I had to decide 'Are we all in, as a company, on cancer?' So we did it, and the Jazz had a phenomenal season last year.

My challenge is for every single company out there to grab "5 For The Fight", put your logo above it, put "5 For The Fight" in your colors, and sponsor a researcher. Do it for someone in your organization that's been affected.[176]

- Salesforce **Pledge 1%:** Pledge 1% is an effort spearheaded by Atlassian, Entrepreneurs Foundation of Colorado, Rally for Impact, Salesforce.org, and Tides to accelerate their shared vision around integrating philanthropy into businesses around the world. Pledge 1% encourages and challenges individuals and companies to pledge 1 percent of equity, product, and employee time for their communities, because committing a small portion of future success can have a significant impact on tomorrow.

  Since launching in 2014, more than 500 companies—from small startups to post-IPO companies—have joined the Pledge 1% movement and committed to making the community a key stakeholder in their businesses. Of the first 500+ companies that have joined the campaign, 59 percent pledged a percentage of equity, 54 percent pledged a percentage of employee time, 39 percent pledged a percentage of the product, and 18 percent pledged a percentage of profit.[177]

- **KIVA:** Kiva is an international nonprofit, founded in 2005 and based in San Francisco, with a mission to connect people through lending to alleviate poverty. They envision a world where all

177 www.pledge1percent.org

people hold the power to create opportunities for themsclves and others. Simplifying the loan industry, Kiva has enabled anyone in the world to lend as little as $25 to anyone else in the world, contributing to the happiness of both the giver and receiver and promoting a better world.

They have created a real movement, with their tagline "Dreams are universal, opportunity is not" and call to action "Compassionate people like you are changing the world." One hundred percent of every dollar you lend on Kiva goes to funding loans. Kiva covers costs primarily through optional donations, as well as through support from grants and sponsors. Kiva lenders crowdfund an average of $2.5 million in loans each week, creating a unique, renewable pool of funds that is reshaping access to financial services around the world. The amount lent through KIVA has already reached one billion dollars with 1.2 million lenders and 2.6 million borrowers (of which 81% are female and 19% male) in 86 countries.

SECTION IV

CLOSING

Drive Happiness G.R.O.W.T.H. in Six Stages

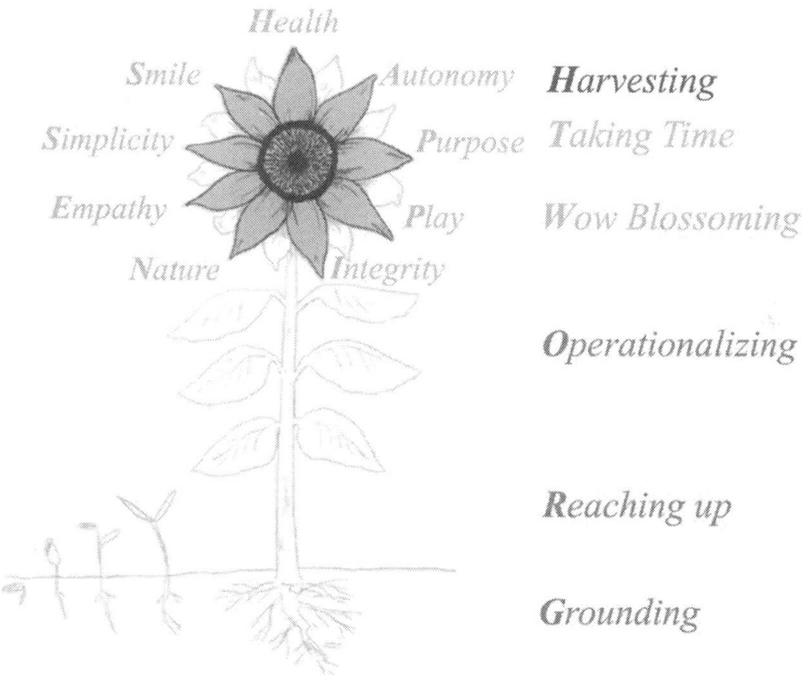

CHAPTER 22

TOP FIVE TAKEAWAYS

"Advice is like aspirin. It tends to only work if you actually take it."

- Dave Murphy

Here are the top five takeaways from *Yellow Factor*:

1. **Seek Happiness First and Profit Will Follow -** If our ultimate purpose in life is to seek happiness and all we all want is happiness, why are we building or working for companies or business models that maximize profits, loyalty, or word of mouth? Why are we not building companies, business models, schools, or universities where the goal is to maximize the happiness of students, teachers, employees, partners, and customers and where profits and loyalty follow as a result? Companies and governmental institutions can leverage nine different ways to contribute to happiness of customers, employees, and society. These ways make the acronym of H.A.P.P.I.N.E.S.S. and are: Health, Autonomy, Purpose, Play, Integrity, Nature, Empathy, Simplicity, and Smile.

2. **Chemicals Drive Happiness -** Happiness comes from specific brain chemicals that evolved to do a job, not to flow all the time for no reason. When we understand their respective roles, we can find healthy new ways to stimulate them. By understanding the six brain molecules linked to happiness, companies can design experiences that achieve both **customer and employee happiness**. **Experiences that release the DOSE neurochemicals make us happy**.

- **D**opamine is your brain's signal that a reward is at hand. The joyful, excited feeling is released when you approach something that meets an unmet need.
- **O**xytocin is the good feeling of social trust. It's released when you find the safety of social support, when you hug someone, or where there is a good touchpoint.
- **S**erotonin is calm confidence in your ability. It's released when you pursue things that reinforce a sense of purpose, meaning, and accomplishment, and when you relax or think of happy memories.
- **E**ndorphin is released when you exercise and when you laugh.

3. Differentiation is Key to Your Growth – It is essential to stand out and differentiate. Happiness offers a competitive advantage because we buy, work, and live to pursue and attain happiness; because we buy *more*, work *better and more effectively,* and live *longer and healthier* lives when we are happy. The search for happiness drives the choices we make due to the chemical wiring of the brain. Even when companies choose other ways than happiness to differentiate themselves, every company and each of us can still have a *Yellow Factor* and **do their little extra that seeds happiness, shines sunlight and contributes to a happier, healthier world**.

4. **Happiness Driven Growth** is a continuous journey across six stages: **G**rounding, **R**eaching-up, **O**perationalizing, **W**ow Blossoming, **T**aking Time, and **H**arvesting.

5. **We Have a Choice -** We can choose a new more sustainable and meaningful way to do business:

- **As company leaders**: how we choose to lead
- **As employees**: how we choose to frame our work and how we choose to design and deliver employee and customer experiences that are meaningful and deliver happiness, or at least comfort, whenever possible
- **As customers**: how we reward (buy, advocate, invest) companies that contribute to happiness and to a better world
- **As human beings**: how we contribute to each other's happiness and whole- being.

CHOOSE HAPPINESS

For us, it ultimately boils down to the question: "*In which world would you rather live? One of pain or one of happiness?*"

We choose **happiness**. And you?

"What will your Yellow Factor be?"

Here's how you can help us create more *Yellow Factor* and spread *Happiness*:

- Apply what you've learned in this book to your brand
- Share the book with others
- Share your favorite quotes on social media using #yellowfactor and #happinessdrivengrowth
- Share with us a photo of you and the book with a glimpse of the country from where you are reading it. On social media, you can use #meandmyyellowfactor #YellowFactorInTheWorld and #YFITW
- Add this book to your company library
- Give this book as a gift to new hires or as present to your employees (or just buy this book for all your employees, if the next festivity is too far away)
- Celebrate International Day of Happiness on March 20
- Bring us in to speak at your conference or company event
- Book us for a workshop, a strategy session or a webinar
- Review this book on Amazon and GoodReads
- Connect with us on *LinkedIn* and *Instagram* and share your thoughts about this book with us. We would love to hear from you!

CHAPTER 23

SUNFLOWERS

"Happiness held is the seed; happiness shared is the flower."

- John Harrigan

TEDx Talk: *Want to be happy? Be grateful* | David Steindl-Rast

25 Smile Quotes about the Value of Smiling:
www.lifehack.org/621816/25-smile-quotes

Remember the sunflowers seeds from AH "*moestuintje*" we spoke about in Nature, and the ones from HelloFresh Mother's Day we wrote about in Smile? Rosaria planted all these seeds in her garden in April, together with her kids. In the same week, Rosaria and Stan had met in Amsterdam to officially kick-off the work on this book. At the end of August, when we sent this book 2018 edition to layout, the seeds had gone through all the stages of Growth. The sunflowers were fully blossoming, had become taller than Rosaria, developed multiple heads (we counted 13 in the most prominent stem), and stood in the garden in all their beauty for the enjoyment of Rosaria's family and every neighbor walking by.

Now that we are writing the 2020 edition, the sunflowers blossoming in Rosaria's garden are actually from the seeds she received from one of her clients. In August 2019, the CEO of Engels & Völker America organized an Elite Retreat on the theme of Happiness for his top 50 employees (an outstanding example of *Yellow Factor* in the categories Smile and Take Time) and invited Rosaria as guest speaker. He also arranged that all the participants would have a yellow welcome bag, featuring a copy of *Yellow Goldfish* and three bags of sunflowers seeds, among many other yellow treats.

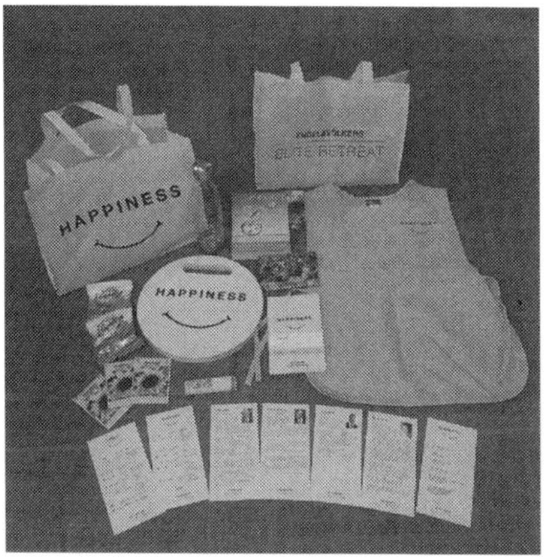

We hope that the insights and tips from this book will help you and your company grow and blossom, and will contribute to your happiness, just as much as blooming sunflowers!

Sunny smiling waves,

Rosaria and Stan

ABOUT THE AUTHORS

STAN PHELPS

Stan Phelps is a best-selling author, keynote speaker, and workshop facilitator. He believes that today's organizations must focus on meaningful differentiation to win the hearts of both employees and customers.

He is the founder of PurpleGoldfish.com. Purple Goldfish is a think tank of customer experience and employee engagement experts that offers keynotes and workshops that drive loyalty and sales. The group helps organizations connect with the hearts and minds of customers and employees.

Prior to PurpleGoldfish.com, Stan had a 20-year career in marketing that included leadership positions at IMG, adidas, PGA Exhibitions, and Synergy. At Synergy, he worked on award-winning experiential programs for top brands such as KFC, Wachovia, NASCAR, Starbucks, and M&M's.

Stan is a TEDx speaker, a Forbes contributor, and IBM Futurist. His writing is syndicated on top sites such as Customer Think and Business2Community. He has spoken at over 300 events across Australia, Bahrain, Canada, Ecuador, France, Germany, Holland, Israel, Japan, Malaysia, Peru, Sweden, Russia, Spain, UK, and the U.S.

He is the author of thirteen books:

- ***Purple Goldfish 2.0*** *– 10 Ways to Attract Raving Fans*
- ***Green Goldfish 2.0*** *- 15 Keys to Driving Employee Engagement*
- ***Golden Goldfish*** *– The Vital Few*
- ***Blue Goldfish*** *- Using Technology, Data and Analytics to Drive Both Profits & Prophets*

- ***Purple Goldfish Service Edition*** - *The 12 Ways Hotels, Restaurants & Airlines Win the Right Customers*
- ***Red Goldfish*** - *Motivating Sales and Loyalty Through Shared Passion & Purpose*
- ***Pink Goldfish*** - *Defy Normal, Exploit Imperfection And Captivate Your Customers*
- ***Purple Goldfish Franchise Edition*** - *The Six Keys to Creating a Successful Franchise S.Y.S.T.E.M.*
- ***Yellow Goldfish*** - *Nine Ways to Increase Happiness in Business for Growth, Productivity, and Prosperity*
- ***Gray Goldfish*** - *Navigating the Gray Areas to Successfully Lead Every Generation*
- ***Red Goldfish Nonprofit Edition*** - *How the Best Nonprofits Leverage Their Purpose to Increase Engagement and Impact*
- ***Diamond Goldfish*** - *Excel Under Pressure & Thrive in the Game of Business*
- ***Silver Goldfish*** - *Loud & Clear: The 10 Keys to Delivering Memorable Presentations*

Stan received a BS in Marketing and Human Resources from Marist College, a JD/MBA from Villanova University, and a certificate for Achieving Breakthrough Service from Harvard Business School. He is a Certified Net Promoter Associate and has taught as an adjunct professor at NYU, Rutgers University, and Manhattanville College. Stan lives in Cary, North Carolina, with his wife, Jennifer, and two boys, Thomas and James.

Stan is also a fellow at Maddock Douglas, an innovation consulting firm in Chicago.

To book Stan for an upcoming keynote, webinar, or workshop, go to stanphelpsspeaks.com. You can reach Stan at stan@purplegoldfish.com or call +1.919.360.4702.

ROSARIA CIRILLO LOUWMAN

Rosaria, an avid learner, is an energetic, enthusiastic, passionate, curious, and driven customer experience professional and happiness change catalyst. Originally from Italy, she graduated *cum laude* from Tor Vergata with a Master in Economics and moved to the Netherlands, where she works and lives since 2002.

Her dream is to live in a world where we all strive to have HAPPY, life-enriching interactions with each other while preserving nature, hence she has made it her mission to bring more happiness and connection into the world through her work.

Rosaria is a TEDx Speaker, CX & Happiness Advisor, Certified Happiness Trainer (CiHS by HSA), Certified Customer Experience Professional (CCXP), former CXPA Authorized Resource Trainer (one of only eight worldwide), and Certified NPS 2 (Net Promoter Score).

In addition to co-authoring *Yellow Goldfish* (now *Yellow Factor*), and translating it to Italian, she is the author of a series of artistic and inspirational books, including *My Circle of Connections* and *Words of Wisdom Nurturing Our World,* both also translated to Italian.

Rosaria has a long history of generating change using Net Promoter and Voice of Customer as a compass to move from data to insight to action to results.

She "walked the talk" for twelve years in sales, e-commerce, and consumer care at leading companies like Forrester, Stream, Adobe, and Philips. In 2013 she started Wow Now on a mission to inspire and empower companies to choose, design, and deliver WOW life-enriching customer experiences that contribute to everyone's HAPPINESS!

She is the developer of the concept of *Happiness Driven Growth©*, a revolutionary business model compelling companies to maximize overall happiness instead of maximizing loyalty and profit. She also developed a new measurement she named *Happiness Contribution™ Factor*.

Since founding Wow Now, she has been advising and inspiring large multinationals like Wolters Kluwer, Heidelberg Drukmachines, and Engels and Völkers, as well as fast-growing medium companies like CustomerGauge, Cleeng, and Voiceworks, and many other companies, including KPN, Nutricia, Aegon, Hello Customer, T-mobile, Enersys, ING, UBM, and MilkyMap about customer experience and happiness through her consultancy, workshops, masterclasses, and public talks.

Rosaria has been a keynote speaker on the concept of Happiness Driven Growth for public events such as TEDx Tor Vergata in Rome, Italy, the World Happiness Summit in Sant Miguel de Allende, Mexico, and the International Workshop on the Science of Happiness in Kharagpur, India. She has spoken at more than 40 in-company events where she has run multiple customer journey mappings, NPS workshops, and countless presentations on the topic of customer experience. She also has facilitated intuitive painting sessions during client off-sites.

An insatiable learner, in 2019, Rosaria has completed a year master program at the Happiness Studies Academy under Tal Ben-Shahar guidance and is now a Certified Happiness Trainer, in addition to having done several masterclasses in the field of Design Thinking and being Certified by the Design Thinkers Academy.

Rosaria lives in Koog aan de Zaan, just outside Amsterdam, with her husband Mathieu and their two sons, Raul and Mauro.

To book Rosaria for an upcoming masterclass, keynote, webinar, or workshop, or event, go to www.wownow.eu. You can find Rosaria on Instagram and Twitter @wownowexp. You can reach Rosaria at rcl@wownow.eu or call +31 6 50924311.

ADDITIONAL INSPIRATION

HAPPINESS CONTRIBUTION™ PODCAST

www.happinesscontribution.com

HAPPINESS DRIVEN GROWTH ASSESSMENT

www.wownow.eu/HappinessGrowthAssessment

HAPPINESS DRIVEN GROWTH TRAILBLAZERS

You can find the most up to date list of trailblazers in this field, and the other links listed below

www.wownow.eu/YellowFactorLinks

Listly Yellow Goldfish collection:

www.list.ly/list/1nzZ-yellow-goldfish-project

Happy songs Spotify playlist:

www.wownow.eu/YGMusicPlaylist

TEDx Talk Playlist

All the TEDx mentioned in this book, and more related to Happiness are available in the YouTube list:

www.wownow.eu/YGTedxHappiness

RECOMMENDED READING

Books on Happiness, Psychology, Leadership, and Self-Development

- *Happier* by Tal Ben-Shahar
- *Nonviolent Communication: A Language of Life* by Marshall Rosenberg
- *Habits of a Happy Brain: Retrain Your Brain to Boost Your Serotonin, Dopamine, Oxytocin and Endorphin Levels* by Loretta Graziano Breuning, PhD
- *10 Keys to Happier Living* by Vanessa King
- *Unlocking Happiness at Work* by Jennifer Moss
- *Start with Why: How Great Leaders Inspire Everyone to Take Action* by Simon Sinek
- *Measuring Happiness* by Joachim Weimann
- *Delivering Happiness* by Tony Hsieh
- *Happiness Advantage: The Seven Principles That Fuel Success and Performance at Work* by Shawn Achor
- *Originals* by Adam Grant
- *Mindset: The New Psychology Of Success - Changing The Way You think To Fulfill Your Potential* by Carol Dweck

- *Thinking, Fast and Slow* by Daniel Kahneman
- *Positive Intelligence* by Shirzad Chamine
- *Daring Greatly* by Brené Brown
- *Rising Strong* by Brené Brown
- *Leadership* by MacGregor Burns
- *The Joy of Leadership* by Tal Ben-Shahar and Angus Ridgway

Books on CX:

- *Would You Do That to Your Mother?* by Jeanne Bliss
- *Chief Customer Officer 2.0: How to Build Your Customer-Driven Growth Engine* by Jeanne Bliss
- *I Love You More Than My Dog* by Jeanne Bliss
- *The Power of Moments: Why Certain Experiences Have Extraordinary Impact* by Dan and Chip Heath
- *Peak* by Chip Conley
- *Made to Stick* by Chip Heath and Dan Heath
- *Outside In: The Power of Putting Customers at the Center of Your Business* by Harley Manning and Kerry Bodine

- *The Ultimate Question 2.0: How Net Promoter Companies Thrive in a Customer-Driven World* by Fred Reichheld and Rob Markey
- *Best Service is No Service* by Bill Price & David Jaffe
- *The Effortless Experience: Conquering the New Battleground for Customer* Loyalty by Matthew Dixon and Nick Toman
- *X: The Experience When Business Meets* Design by Brian Solis
- *The Purple Cow* by Seth Godin

Books on Design Thinking:

- *Service Design for Business* by Ben Reason, Lavrans Lovlie, Melvin Brand Flu
- *Gamestorming: A Playbook for Innovators, Rulebreakers, and Changemakers* by Dave Gray, Sunni Brown, James Macanufo
- *This is Service Design Thinking: Basics, Tools, Cases* by Mark Stickdorn and Jakob Schneider
- *This Is Service Design Doing: Applying Service Design and Design Thinking in the Real World* by Marc Stickdorn and Markus Edgar Hormes

Printed by Amazon Italia Logistica S.r.l.
Torrazza Piemonte (TO), Italy

46522934R00160